Published by Jolo Press

Copyright © 1968 Joan Lock
All rights reserved

Joan Lock has asserted her right
under the Copyright, Designs and Patents Act 1988
to be identified as the author of this work

ISBN-13 978-1-51220-834-4

Also available as a Kindle ebook
ISBN-13 978-1-84396-363-9

A CIP catalogue record for this
book is available from the British Library.

This book is sold subject to the condition that it
shall not, by way of trade or otherwise, be lent, resold, hired
out, or otherwise circulated without the author's prior
consent in any form of binding or cover other than that in
which it is published and without a similar condition being
imposed on the subsequent purchaser.

Pre-press production
eBook Versions
127 Old Gloucester Street
London WC1N 3AX
www.ebookversions.com

Other books by Joan Lock

NON-FICTION

Blue Murder?
Dreadful Deeds & Awful Murders
Marlborough Street: The Story of a London Court
Reluctant Nightingale
Scotland Yard Casebook
Scotland Yard's First Cases
Tales from Bow Street
The British Policewoman: Her Story
The Princess Alice Disaster

FICTION

Dead Image
Dead Born
Dead Letters
Dead Loss
Dead Fall
Dead End
Dead Centre
Death in Perspective

Acknowledgements

Miss Christine Kerridge: For her help
in the verification of facts and for the use of
her remarkable memory for detail.

My husband: For his constructive
criticism and invaluable assistance in
editing this book.

LADY POLICEMAN

Joan Lock

JOLO PRESS

1
'What about the offence, Officer?'

'Officer, there is a laundry basket in the middle of Bond Street,' said a public-spirited citizen as he passed me. After I had digested this fascinating piece of information I proceeded in a determined, though not too brisk manner, in the direction of the said basket. Perhaps it would go away before I got there.

But no, there it was, a very large laundry basket smack in the middle of the junction with Brook Street. What's more it was full to the brim with clean laundry – sheets, pillowcases, towels and pyjamas.

'Anyone know where it came from?' I asked the interested onlookers. A shaking of heads. I prodded my memory for instructions so recently learned at preliminary training school. Property found – 'a note in your pocket book signed by the finder, then take the property to the station.' Take it to the station! That was at least a quarter of a mile away and the basket weighed a ton. Surely I couldn't tie up the station van for something so unimportant.

A label on the basket gave the name of Lord Blank and an address much nearer than the 'nick'. I could use the alternative procedure – 'If you are satisfied that a claimant owns the property you may hand it over against his signature after getting permission from the station officer.'

'Would you help me carry this basket to the owner?' I asked a rather charming, interested onlooker.

'Certainly officer, I'm going that way anyway.'

As we threaded our way through the elegant shoppers I chatted with my gallant assistant and tried to give the impression that it was the most normal thing in the world for a Woman Police Constable to lug a laundry basket through Mayfair. It was further than we realised and we arrived pink and panting at the Lord's abode. A surprised caretaker informed us; 'His Lordship is on the French Riviera where he is liable to remain for the next four weeks at least.'

Oh damn! Still the caretaker should suffice as a signatory. I phoned my sergeant who consented – provided that everything was itemised. I was soon, with a bemused caretaker, knee-deep in the Lord's smalls. He did not know why the laundry should be littering Bond Street but today was delivery day – perhaps it had been lost en route.

Back at the nick the station officer was very cross. A worried van driver and his mate had just reported the loss of one basket of laundry they had no idea where or when but thought it must have fallen from the back of the van.

'They've gone now and it's all in the property book. How am I going to get a signature against it?' he grumbled. 'Why didn't you ring for the van, and who gave' you permission to hand it over?'

'Well, I didn't want to bother you so I asked my Woman Police Sergeant.'

'You shouldn't have. I'm in charge here.'

It transpired that he was making much ado about nothing and the sacred property book could be 'squared up' with just a little more bother than usual.

So I had not done so badly after all. I would go and have a cup of tea. The Sergeant's voice stopped me.

'What are you doing about the offence?'

'Offence, Sarge?'

'Dangerous load, my girl, dangerous load. That flying basket could have killed someone. Oh, go and have a cup of tea.'

A few days later I was strolling down Charing Cross Road and wallowing in the rare spring sunshine when a little old man panted up to me.

'Come quickly, miss. A bloke's collapsed in the pub – I think he's dying.'

Ah, this was more in my line after four years' nursing and a recently acquired State Registration. Not that I was particularly good at first aid. Like most nurses I was used to working under instruction and with the right equipment. But I was used to sick people and first aid for most collapse cases was straightforward and minimal.

The patient, a heavily-built old man, was lying on a bench in the public bar with several of the inevitable onlookers hovering around him. He was unconscious, his breathing stertorous, and his occasional involuntary movements made it apparent that he was partially paralysed. I diagnosed a stroke, loosened his clothing at neck, chest and waist, removed his false teeth and positioned his head so that he would not swallow his tongue.

'You've phoned for an ambulance?' I asked.

'Well, no. We thought we'd wait for a policeman.'

They were trying to undress the old man when I returned.

'I told you to leave him alone, there is nothing you can do. He is best kept still.'

They looked doubtful. What did this young girl know? Obviously they must do *something*.

'We must at least take off his overcoat and shoes,' said a spokesman.

'No. I'm a state registered nurse and I know what I'm talking about. The ambulance will be here soon.'

I was trying to assert my authority but merely sounded prim and cold. However, they were placated for a while except one man who kept muttering, 'Should at least take his shoes off.'

The patient's condition appeared to be worsening and the ambulance was taking longer than anticipated. The onlookers were getting restless again and, doubt being very contagious, I began to wonder if there *was* something I had forgotten. The mutterer started to pull at the old man's shoelaces.

'Oh all right, take them off – gently, mind.'

I don't know what this did for the patient but it certainly made the remover much happier and gave me some peace until those marvellously matter-of-fact ambulance men arrived.

I took the first of many rides in with the patient. The antiseptic smells and the self-important bustle of the hospital staff made me feel nostalgic. I cured myself quickly by remembering the awful conditions of employment, the bitchiness of fellow staff and the complete disregard for my health and comfort which I had endured in the nursing profession. By comparison police conditions, though irksome to some, seemed to me a paradise of leisure, esprit de corps, wealth and paternalism.

'I have all the man's personal details but the doctor said he would let us have the diagnosis later. It's probably a stroke,' I told the station officer grandly.

'You were wrong miss,' he said a little while later, 'it was an apoplectic fit.'

'Same thing given its technical term,' I said casually. He was impressed but not finished.

'What were those people doing in licensed premises at that hour of the day?'

'I don't know, Sir, I never asked them.'

'Well you should have. There could be an offence there, you know.'

I went for a cup of tea.

2
Toms

Though the basic work of a police officer is the same all over the world, there are many variations which are governed by local geography and social conditions. The more extreme examples are the country copper who supervises sheep dips and the towny who copes with organised vice. But there are many more subtle differences which can lead to a quite different work load in apparently similar areas.

For instance, a hospital on the division means more accident investigations, suicide reports and aliens' enquiries (concerning the hospital's domestic employees). A railway terminus will bring more casual callers to the station for accommodation advice whilst local tourist attractions will involve the beat policeman in much direction-giving very wearing on the voice and the index finger. Traffic is heavier in the cities but also much slower, so a quiet country road is more likely to produce a really serious accident. Ironically the ambulance gets to the city accident within minutes. In more isolated spots it may take up to an hour or more. Sexual offences too are more common in rural and suburban areas. Lonely roads and wide open spaces aid their commission. But city parks also have their share of 'flashing' (indecent exposure), buggery and indecent assault. Wicked Soho is far safer for the innocent bystander.

The special features of police work in London's West End were dealing with offences committed by prostitutes, shoplifters, street traders, buskers and street photographers; handling the heavy traffic with its few serious accidents but many 'touches; supervising and prosecuting where necessary the numerous clubs and licensed premises and finding some of the runaway juveniles and approved school absconders who made for the bright lights. There was also crowd control at ceremonial events and premieres and giving assistance to and acting as photographic models for tourists. (Unofficial this one.) Plenty of work too for the CID of course, stealing from unattended cars being the worst crime headache.

But among all this variety one subject was of most abiding interest and fascination to the public – prostitution. Thus the stock introduction, 'This is Joan, she is a lady policeman in the West End' produced interested noises promptly followed by, 'You must have your work cut out with "the girls".' Or, 'Do the "pros" give you a lot of trouble?' in suitably confidential tones.

'Pros' and 'the girls' were terms they fondly imagined to be common police parlance. In fact we never used them. A prostitute was a 'tom' or just a prostitute and to practice prostitution was 'tomming', being 'on the game', 'on the batter' or just plain soliciting – all expressions used by the prostitutes themselves.

The toms were as mixed in type as humans anywhere. There was the caricature with brassy blonde hair, tight skirt, jutting bosom and loud, vulgar mouth. The small, businesslike, smartly suited and well corseted continental who usually worked regular hours and visited the VD clinic equally regularly. A few Mayfair toms with their beautiful clothes, excellent taste and manners looked and often acted more like the popular idea of a 'lady' than many a bona fide lady in the area. Then, finally, the enthusiastic amateur who was openly despised by the professional. She was usually young, rather scruffy, and hung around where she was most likely to pick up casual male acquaintances, often American servicemen or lonely foreigners. Her favours were exchanged for a bed and a few meals though I doubt whether this bargain was made in so many words. Many still harboured vaguely romantic ideas about their benefactors and would have been surprised and offended by the word 'prostitute'.

Of course, these are generalisations there were dozens of other types and mutations. Some were intelligent, more were stupid, some very beautiful, others ravaged and ugly, some out of whose mouths obscenities poured, others who would not dream of using the mildest swear word, some who would come quietly and others who would always create havoc as a matter of principle. Many were saving up to retire when the 1959 Street Offences Act came into force. I thought it would be interesting to see which type survived. My bet was on the business-like continental and the Mayfair tom, most of whom had a nucleus of regular clients who called on the same day, same time, each week. Sex by appointment.

*   *   *

I met Mabel in the charge room about four months after my arrival at West End Central. She was one of the ravaged kind. Her bloated, shiny-pink face with its piggy eyes, sparse eyebrows and sloppy mouth, was surrounded by yellow sausage curls and frizz. She stank of body odour, cheap perfume, even cheaper booze, and was very drunk. Her wandering eyes found me, stopped to focus and stayed to grow belligerent. I was standing beside the charge desk ready to assist Matron should Mabel prove difficult. The severe uniform with its flattering white starched collar had the effect of making a young face look younger and a pure expression purer. I was young (21), quite pretty and had (I was told) a very demure expression. A red rag to a bull.

She screamed with derisive laughter and pointed at me.

'Miss Bleeding Purity, don't look down your nose at me! You know your fucking trouble, you've never had it.' (She was right there.) I assumed my impervious, heard-it-all-before expression. But – I blushed. As usual, I pretended it wasn't happening while the colour crept slowly up my neck and spread all over my face. Mabel was delighted and went in for the kill.

'Nobody would fancy a prune-faced old cow like you,' she cackled.

'Here, why don't you have a bash at her that would take that bloody expression off her face,' she addressed herself to an obviously mortified young PC who pretended he had not heard and looked everywhere but at me.

The station officer glanced up briefly from his charge book.

'That's enough of that, this is a police station,' he said sternly. Drunks are often like children divert their attention and they will quickly forget their original obsession. Mabel's attention was promptly switched to the station officer, and after abusing him mildly for a while she lapsed into silence. I tried to relax my facial expression without being too obvious about it so that next time her gaze wobbled in my direction I wouldn't trigger off a stream of obscenities. But she forgot about me until I assisted Matron to 'put her down'.

'Get your bleeding hands off of me, you lesbian,' she screamed, pushing me away. She continued her tirade all the way to the cell. As we left she had her final word.

'Perhaps you haven't got one!'

The thought amused her greatly.

* * *

That scene, with slight variations, was repeated several times during my career. Though there seemed to be some divergence of opinion as to whether I had never had 'it' and was jealous or had had 'it' and was trying to pretend that I had not. But on one point there was complete accord, I was a lesbian.

Every new prostitute on the ground had her 'dabs' (fingerprints) and antecedents, taken by a WPC which were then sent to Criminal Record Office at the Yard for checking. The antecedents form was a lengthy questionnaire on past employments, schools, residences and a detailed physical description. Although the women were often initially recalcitrant towards us, this 'stripping-down' procedure seemed to act like a confessional and they soon became more relaxed and confiding. I usually encouraged this as I never saw much point in acting 'holier than thou', an attitude which made the prisoner uncooperative and the job more difficult. The trick was to retain control without being condescending or over familiar. In fact, after memory-prodding and getting all black-fingered together with one of the brighter types, a camaraderie sometimes developed. A bouncy colleague having struck up such a temporary 'friendship' was having difficulty elucidating the girl's natural hair colour.

'Let's have a look at the roots,' she said, reaching out and touching the hair. The whole scalp slipped askew. It was a wig and the girl was a boy. Panic ensued. 'She', had already been charged with soliciting prostitution although we could hardly be blamed for that. We couldn't start sexing the prisoners.

But on another occasion I was judge and jury in just such a sexing. Fortunately it was before the prisoner had been charged. A group of prostitutes had been arrested together.

'Will you have a look at the blonde?' said the arresting officer. 'She's new and the other girls say she is a man.'

The blonde was tall and slim, she wore a tightly fitting sweater which showed up her very good bust-line, a full skirt puffed out with many petticoats and teetering high heels. The bleached hair was long and bouffant with flicked-up ends and was obviously her own. Her face was longish and heavily made-up. The only suspect details were the rather strong angles of the face and ankles and a slight coarseness of the complexion.

I took her into a detention room – the matron, a gossipy woman, came with us. To save the prisoner a lot of embarrassment I asked her point-blank if she was a man. She denied it vehemently – but in a dark brown voice.

'Right, lift up your jumper and undo your bra,' I said briskly. Her chest was quite flat like a man's, not a sign of a breast. The good bust-line was completely false. She still insisted she was a woman. Though I thought the evidence pretty conclusive, I was uneasy at making a pronouncement on such a limited examination. She just might be a hermaphrodite.

'I'm not quite satisfied, would you prefer a doctor to examine you further?'

'Oh no, I'd rather you did it,' she said nervously. Lift up your skirt then, please.'

I wished Matron would not watch so avidly. The brief panties presented a flat front – no help at all. There was only one thing to do. I put my hand between her legs and made my decision. She was a man – clinically anyway. The male organs were there all right but strapped back so as not to show. She broke down then and admitted her sex but insisted that she wanted to be a woman and was undergoing a sex change. I assured her that the Court would take this into consideration. Whilst feeling very sorry for him/her I did wonder what sort of clients he/she was soliciting for and if they knew what they were getting.

When I left the detention room Matron was already regaling a group of PCs with details of how I had touched 'it'. She was quite pink in the face and giggling helplessly. The story went the rounds, no doubt well embroidered, and I endured the inevitable ribbing.

Most of the prostitutes were arrested by a special patrol in which about ten officers operated in pairs. Male officers were discouraged from making lone arrests due to the very real risk of allegations by some prostitutes. The woman was often taken to the station in a taxi. A strange procedure with a prisoner you might think, but a practical one. Prostitute arrests were too numerous to allow the use of the van for each one. There was only the alternative of walking to the nick. This was disliked by the women because it was tiring in stiletto heels, time-wasting, and exposed them to the gawping public. The arresting officers also disliked it because a long walk with a prisoner increases the risk of escape or of involvement in other incidents en route. And they didn't like the gawping public either.

Who paid the fare? The prostitute did. Usually as soon as arrested she would say, 'Let's get a cab'. Only if she had been particularly difficult might the officer insist that they walk or wait for the van. But tit for tat sometimes, the women furious at being arrested would say, 'I'm not paying for a cab, I want the van.' Or, 'I'll make you walk.'

Whichever it was she usually walked fast.

Relationships between the regular offenders and the policeman are much more friendly than is generally realised. The intimacy of the cab trips soon got the women talking and some eye-opening tales they had to tell. Apparently a high percentage of their clients were requested practices so far removed from sexual intercourse that I think it would be perfectly possible to be a prostitute and remain a virgin – provided she was selective!

But a cab trip was nearly my undoing. It was the practice for the cabs to wait outside the station while the prostitute was charged and bailed - rarely more than twenty minutes. I had arrested Gerda, a German prostitute renowned for her uncertain temper and her sexy skin-tight trousers (we used to speculate on how many 'man-hours' she wasted getting them on and off). There had been an order that cabs must no longer be allowed to wait but must be paid off. This was gradually falling into abeyance as these things are wont to do – so when Gerda pleaded to keep the cab I foolishly consented without much ado.

The station officer charged her and then said, 'Right lass, put her down for a couple of hours and check her address – it hasn't been checked for a long time.' Oh Lord, I thought, what about the cab fare? I consulted Gerda in the cell.

'Take it out of my property,' she said.

'Don't be silly Gerda, you know that can't be touched until you are bailed,' I said irritably.

She shrugged, 'I don't know then.'

I knew that the cabbie would be equally unmoved by my plight. I was willing to fork out just to get out of a hole, but didn't want to get financially involved with a prostitute. Still, there was no other alternative – I paid and informed Gerda.

'I will give it to you at Court in the morning,' she said.

'Oh that won't be necessary,' I said casually, 'forget it.' My God, she might as well sell tickets!

'Of course I will give it to you,' she said stiffly, 'I do not owe money to anyone.'

The following morning I saw her across the courtroom but managed to avoid speaking to her.

It was several weeks before I saw her again and I had in fact forgotten the incident. But she had not. I was patrolling Mayfair when she approached me.

'Wait a minute, please,' she said in her guttural accent and dashed to her nearby flat.

'What on earth does she want?' asked my patrolling companion.

'Oh dear, I've just remembered, I think she wants to give me some money.'

'Well don't just stand there. Quick, let's go!'

But it was too late, Gerda had returned and was insistently pressing several shillings into my palm. I pocketed the money, thanked her briefly and fled the scene of 'bribery and corruption'. I heard nothing more of the incident but realised that it was not only the male officers who should be cautious with prostitutes.

Later in my service it became fashionable for prostitutes to solicit from cars. Trickier to arrest. Being a person who always has to learn the hard way I arrested one such – and then accepted her invitation to drive me to the nick. She had argued logically enough that she would have to drive me around until she found a parking place (once arrested I couldn't let her out of my sight) and then find transport to the station so why not? I soon found out why not – she was a bloody awful driver. Was my face red sitting beside her with my imagination working overtime!

'...And how was it, Officer, that you were on duty and sitting beside the driver, a common prostitute, at the time of the accident?'

'Well, er, actually she was under arrest, Sir...'

But luck was with me and we made it to the station unscathed – physically anyway!

One sunny, summer afternoon I even posed as a prostitute. With the 'New Act' looming in the near future there had been an increase of newsagents' notice-board ads for 'Models', 'French Lessons', 'Swedish Masseuse', 'Strict Governess' etc. Our hierarchy wanted to keep an eye on this trend. There was much speculation at the time on what was going to happen when prostitution was driven underground. So I was requested to visit all businesses displaying such boards and ask how much they would charge for such a notice.

It was a doubtful honour being asked to represent the oldest profession and I wondered if it was the result of a rather disastrous 'red rinse' given me on my last visit to the hairdressers. The colour didn't take too kindly to my currently fashionable salmon-pink duster coat.

I'm a dreadful actress but my 'non-police' appearance usually got me by on such occasions. Nonetheless I was highly embarrassed when after asking the cost of an ad' insertion the proprietor looked at me closely and said, 'What sort of ad'?'

'Model.'

And the other occupants of the shop turned to have a good look at me with my red hair, pink coat and demure expression. I thought to myself, 'The blooming things I do for this job!'

The answer was anything from thirty shillings to fifty shillings per week. So a board with about ten ads would provide a weekly income of up to £25 not bad at all!

But I decided that the profession was not for me I hadn't the nerve. I would stick to my own kind of street walking in future.

3
Stops

The mainstay of women police work in the West End was 'stops in the street'. The Metropolitan Police used two Acts of Parliament which gave them this power. The Metropolitan Police Act gave them right to stop, search and detain a person reasonably suspected of having stolen property whilst the Children and Young Persons Act allowed the stopping of suspected juvenile absconders.

We women police made most use of the Children and Young Persons Act. These stops winkled out the juveniles who had absconded from approved schools, Borstals, Fit Person, Supervision or Probation Orders, or were missing from home. There were people who thought that this stopping business was an intolerable assault on liberty and privacy and 'ought not to be allowed' – obviously it was only an outlet for police power mania. They were usually the same people who cried 'something should be done about all this crime and juvenile delinquency'. But those who think that one can make omelettes without breaking eggs will always be with us.

Looking at a crowded West End street and it might seem impossible to single out anyone from the throng. But practice, an observant eye and nerve worked wonders. Some women police became aces at this. I was not one of them. I lacked the nerve. What did we look for? Firstly, youthful appearance especially if the hour was late. Then a grubby and unkempt look particularly around the feet and legs. Scuffed and dirty shoes, laddered stockings or none at all, often indicated that a girl had been sleeping rough. Sometimes at close quarters the smell was also indicative.

Attitude was important. A girl who didn't want to be noticed either tried to get out of our sight quickly or brazened it out by approaching us and asking the way, assuming we would be fooled by this. Only the iron-nerved, or the girl new to the West End who did not expect our attentions, managed to ignore our existence.

Once we had decided on our girl we approached her and, mustering our most tactful manner, said something like this:

'Excuse me, may I just have a word with you please?' and, if possible, ushered her into a nearby doorway away from interested onlookers. If there were two of us and two girls we separated them for questioning and then compared their stories.

Occasionally, as soon as the girl spoke we realised we had made a mistake. The 'scruff' might merely be an arty or beat type who deliberately looked scruffy and the very young face could belong to a grown woman. In that case we tactfully apologised and let her go. If we had behaved politely and explained the reasons for the intrusion into their privacy most people were quite reasonable.

In the other cases we started with a few simple questions. 'What is your name? How old are you? What's your date of birth? Where do you live?'

The age question was most important because when under seventeen the girl was legally a juvenile and as such warranted our attention even if not an absconder. The girls were only too well aware of the seventeen-year deadline so immediately gave their ages as seventeen or over. That was why we followed with, 'What's your date of birth?' Few girls were quick enough to alter the birth date to match the age they had given. So we neatly caught them out – in theory that is – in fact I am so dense at the simplest of maths that I often wasn't quick enough either. Whilst assuming my best 'nothing escapes me' expression I was vainly trying to work out the date (whether she had had her birthday that year is crucial) and longing to use my fingers.

Being under seventeen in the West End was no crime of course but if the girl was caught out by lying about her age we knew that there was probably more to it than that.

To check the name and address we would ask the girl to look in her handbag to see if she had any proof of identity. She would probably tell us she had nothing. We would ask her to check to make sure. Once her bag was open we might see an envelope whose existence she couldn't then deny or sometimes we could reach casually into the bag and say, 'Oh look, how about this?' If the correspondence was in a different name or maybe even one we recognised as that of an absconder or missing person, it was usually being 'kept for a friend'.

Even a birth certificate or an insurance card was no real proof of identity as the girls used to borrow or steal them from each other. We became quite familiar with some documents as they passed from hand to hand. One particular favourite had a Christian name of Queen Mary. Not very unobtrusive.

Further general questioning gave us a better opportunity to weigh up the girl's character and manner and to judge if her story was feasible. But there are few police officers who have not been taken in by a good liar. Like a magistrate they have to try to ignore the honest, pleasant and convincing manner so as to concentrate on the facts. This is where experience really tells. Initially, I was a trusting, gullible little soul who did not tell lies and could see no reason why anyone else should do so.

In my early days whilst I was being 'carried' I listened in on my first stop. It was performed by Marge, a serious ex-school teacher with a rather preoccupied manner. I was a bit embarrassed by her stopping a girl who, to me, was quite respectable-looking and harming no one. I thought the girl was being very nice about it all. Surely it was obvious that she was telling the truth? She had such a frank, open manner and she looked over eighteen as well. I was shocked when Marge said in her slightly abrupt way, 'I'm not quite satisfied with your story. Will you come to the phone-box with me so that I can check a little further, please?'

I was very pleasant to the girl on the way to the police box at Piccadilly Circus to make up for my colleague's overzealousness. No wonder we got complaints! Marge, noting my puzzled expression muttered briefly, 'She's lying'.

We did a routine check with the index at the Yard where details were kept of wanted or missing juveniles. It included name, aliases, birthday and scar indexes. Whether we got a 'match' might depend on the intuition and thoroughness of the person at the other end.

Tying up descriptions was the trickiest thing. Often a file description might be out of date, poor, or even quite wrong on some details, especially if given by the relative of a missing girl. Most people are very unobservant about physical details and relatives rarely seem to take a good look at each other. 'Tall' or 'short' often depends on the height of the person who is doing the estimating using themselves as a yardstick.

Girls can alter their appearance quite drastically by changing the style, cut or colour of their hair, by wearing different clothes or even a height of heel that varies from their normal wear. Scars, tattoos or birthmarks were invaluable as identifiers because of their permanence (except when removed by thoughtful prison surgeons).

Marge had no luck on the phone and this is where the crunch always came. Did we let her go even though not really happy about her or did we take the bigger step of asking her to come to the police station for further enquiries? There was always the chance that she would refuse. How forceful were we prepared to be on the evidence available? (A girl once lay down on the pavement in the middle of busy Tottenham Court Road and screamed her head off when I asked her to come to the station. Not one of my better moments.) If things went wrong it would be our heads that would roll.

I was appalled by Marge's decision to take her to the nick. The girl was now being a bit less co-operative and I didn't blame her. At West End Central we phoned the local police and asked them to check at her home. The reply which came an hour later was to become very familiar during my service.

'Not known at the address given.'

'They must have gone to Sheldon Street instead of Sheldon Avenue,' said the girl nonchalantly.

Sometime later when she realised that we were as determined as she was, she finally admitted to being an approved school absconder. I was shattered but learning.

But it was not always as simple as that. Girls soon learned that our quickest way of verification was to do a 'home check'. So the experienced ones 'killed off' their parents, guardians and any close relatives (some even hammed up the orphaned-and-all-alone-in-the-world act). This made it more difficult for us but it also made us more certain of our ground. Some were such hard nuts that they would never admit who they were, even when faced with irrefutable evidence such as a perfect photographic likeness or when confronted with a relative.

'That's not my mother,' said one stony-faced girl. While Mum, who had been brought down from Scotland to identify her, stood with the tears streaming down her face saying, 'Yes, that's my daughter.'

One particular girl caught me out beautifully regarding her identification. We had had a message to keep our eyes open for two escapees from a certain approved school which seemed to have more girls on the loose than inside. It was sometimes easier to catch them when they were fresh out as they needed time to make contacts, get a place to sleep and a change of clothes. In this instance my patrolling companion and I knew one of the girls – one Helen Rogers. We were making our way towards a notorious dive which provided us with plenty of work in the shape of young mysteries when two CID 'aides' rushed past us and gasped, Two girls went the other way when they saw you. We're going round the back to head them off.'

The rear view of the girls who were now fast disappearing down a short side street was the first we had seen of them. They looked back, saw our rapid approach and started to run straight into the arms of the CID. They put up quite an energetic fight for liberty. One was Helen Rogers. We took them to the nearby police section house to await the van.

'You of course are Jenny Roberts, the girl who escaped with Helen,' I said to the other girl. She looked blank. 'Never heard of her, my name's Rosemary Smythe.' I looked at her with disbelief.

'That's right,' said Helen, 'Jenny and I split up as soon as we escaped. Thought we'd have a better chance that way. I met Rosemary in the club.'

It was true that girls often did split up so as to be less recognisable. But I didn't believe them this time. It seemed too much of a coincidence that she'd chummed up with another girl so quickly. I checked with the Yard and to my surprise the answer came back, 'Yes, Rosemary Smythe is on licence from a school in Yorkshire. If she's down here she must have absconded.'

That settled it she wouldn't claim to be a girl who might be wanted – no point in that.

Next morning Helen was duly collected. Early in the afternoon the phone rang in the Women Police room. It was the front office.

'Your escort from Yorkshire is here to collect Smythe.'

'O.K., I'll come down and see her.'

Before I was out of the door the phone rang again.

'This is the Approved School. We brought Helen Rogers back today and she was giggling all the way. When we got here she finally told us the joke. The girl who was arrested with her *was* Jenny Roberts.'

I was astonished.

'But why give the name of a girl who is on licence?'

'No idea, she's a bit odd.'

I went to the juvenile detention room and challenged the girl.

'I *am* Rosemary Smythe,' she said stubbornly.

'We'll soon see.'

I fetched the escort.

'I'm afraid there may have been a bit of a *faux pas*,' I said. 'Do you know Smythe?'

'Oh yes, very well.'

'Is this her?' I said opening the door.

'Oh no. That's not Rosemary.'

'Yes I *am*,' said the girl defiantly.

My temper was beginning to fray at the edges.

'Don't be so stupid! This lady knows Rosemary Smythe well. Don't you realise you've dragged her on a wild goose chase all the way from Yorkshire? We know you are Jenny Roberts.'

'No I'm not,' she said, giving me the unblinking, stony stare. I choked on my temper and left the detention room quickly. I'd never laid a finger on anyone in custody but I was sorely tempted to give her a back-hander.

Later I coldly informed her that she would be collected as soon as we could get another escort from her approved school. She started to cry.

'Why don't you want to go back?' I asked, softening a bit. 'I'm the only virgin there and the other girls make fun of me.'

The belligerent facade was gone.

'Why on earth did you give the name of a girl who would be wanted?'

'My mate met the girl in an approved school and she knew she'd been let out since. We didn't realise she might be on licence.'

In case the subtlety of this misses you if she had given the name of a girl of whom we had no trace I would have obviously pressed my enquiries. By giving a 'known but not wanted' name (so she thought) I would then let her go.

'I'm sorry about this,' I said to the escort. 'It's my fault – one should never presume anything.'

'Think nothing of it,' she said cheerily, 'it makes a change to come down here and gives me the chance to do some Christmas shopping. I won't have to escort a truculent girl on the return journey either.'

Well, at least *she* was happy!

On two occasions I was able to arrest an absconder because she kept an appointment. We often received information of a date a girl might be keeping but we usually waited in vain for them to appear. Such information filtered back from various sources, sometimes from remand homes and approved schools – girls splitting on their mates, or conversations overheard by the staff. One day we were tipped off that an absconder from a supervision order would be outside a cafe near Piccadilly Circus at 2 p.m. to keep a date. The description was rather scanty: tall, red hair, brown eyes, dress unknown. Could be anybody except for one other detail – she was said to be strikingly ugly.

Two of us were outside the cafe in plain clothes well before the appointed time, expecting another vain wait. But on the dot a tall, red-haired girl appeared. It seemed ludicrous to identify her this way but she *was* strikingly ugly her face being long and horsy and features heavy. There were the usual denials but we were quite sure this was our girl.

On the way to the nick we gave her a pep talk about going straight, especially now her supervision order was nearly finished.

'You can save your sermons for someone else,' she said without malice. 'I intend to be a prostitute and nothing you or anyone else says will stop me.'

The quiet determination and finality in her voice shut us up.

Who could blame her?

The second girl arrested was an absconder from an approved school whom I had originally dealt with for Care or Protection. Our information came from the school. Girls were encouraged to form attachments to members of the staff (in the purest way) to give them an anchor. This girl – Julie – had escaped and then phoned her particular attachment and asked her to meet her where the World met - outside Swan and Edgar's at Piccadilly Circus. This put the woman in an unenviable position. She liked the girl and valued her trust but owed her allegiance to the school, so had no choice but to inform the headmistress of the assignation.

The teacher insisted on accompanying us.

'Let me speak to her first,' she said, 'I don't want to destroy her trust completely. She's intelligent and has been doing so well studying for her GCEs. The trouble is she's got no conception of right and wrong and there's not much we can do about that.'

I remembered Julie as a scruffy young girl (15 years) who made such funny remarks when I was taking her statement that I had to stare icily at a young WPC who was 'sitting in' to stop her from giggling.

The front of Swan and Edgar became more and more crowded as the time approached and the worried teacher became more and more concerned. We waited apart from her so that Julie would not weigh up the situation and flit before we saw her. At ten minutes past the hour she had not arrived. I was trying to conceal myself in case she recognised me and at the same time look everywhere among the crowds hoping I would recognise her. I expected her to sidle up to her friend but I had not taken her strange character into account. Suddenly, bounding into view, came a smart blonde, dressed in green with a matching umbrella held aloft. Other eyes besides ours turned to watch her progress. She couldn't have made a more brazen entrance.

We allowed the teacher to speak first but we were close behind and Julie was too quick not to realise what was happening. She 'had a go for it' – completely denying her identity and playing the outraged innocent. But she soon had the sense to see it was futile. After the initial shock she soon recovered her sense of humour and started to make the most of being the centre of attention once again. The unhappy teacher was ignored.

I complimented Julie on her appearance. She grinned.

'I don't sleep rough any more. I've learnt a thing or two since you nicked me. I've got places to go now.' She mused a while.

'What a state I was in that first time, remember?'

I congratulated myself on my achievement.

'Dear old West End Central, Home Sweet Home,' she said as we approached that ugly building. Her gaiety and humour were hard to resist. By the time she left for the approved school she was even beginning to thaw towards the errant teacher.

'She does take it all to heart so,' Julie confided.

As I have said, some WPCs became 'stop aces'. The best I ever knew was June, a shrewd cockney with a classic face and slim figure which could have graced a fashion magazine had she been more interested in her appearance. She had an unerring eye for a good stop, an uncanny instinct for sensing when a girl was telling lies and sufficient confidence in her judgement to carry the job through. It was June who brought a mum down from Scotland on pretty flimsy evidence because she was sure in her own mind that a girl who had been brought in for prostitution was a certain missing girl!

One night a group of us girls from West End Central was on one of its intermittent dinner and theatre jaunts. We had enjoyed the show and were heading towards chicken chop-suey when we passed one of those glass-fronted coffee bars near Leicester Square. It was one of our hunting grounds and by reflex action we all peered in as we passed.

June (who also had a photographic memory for faces) said casually, 'I'm sorry, girls, there's an absconder sitting in there and I just can't ignore her. Won't take us long to get her to the nick and the reserve can take care of most of the details.'

We appreciated that she couldn't just ignore the girl – and after all, it was rarely this easy.

The absconder must have thought that the day of judgement had come when she walked along Coventry Street surrounded by a posse of women police in plain clothes. Fortunately the van was standing at Piccadilly Circus. We decided to stick together, so all trooped up the steep steps with unaccustomed difficulty in our high heels and slim skirts.

The formalities were quickly accomplished and soon we were off out again and well into our sweet and sour.

I spent one tour of duty lying in wait for an absconder in her flat. She had been arrested for prostitution but it only became known to us after she left Court that she *was* an absconder (juveniles were not normally fingerprinted so the usual dabs check at the Yard was useless in this case). We did have an address though it was doubtful she would return there. Two of us were assigned to her flat just in case.

It was one of those tiny bed-sit and kitchen flats up rickety wooden stairs in an old house. We were admitted by a huge red-haired maid. Many prostitutes employ maids to help safeguard them from difficult and/or violent clients as well as to do some cleaning. Some are ex-prostitutes well past their prime.

The stairs led straight into the main room and at the top, looking aggressive, stood the biggest boxer dog I have ever seen. I was pleased when the maid shooed him out of the way.

'He's very friendly,' she cackled.

We searched the girl's scant belongings to see if we could find any information or addresses. There was nothing but a few clothes and a bundle of obscene photographs which made my eyes pop (prostitutes often used these to accelerate their clients). They depicted intercourse and attendant features from various positions and angles and some I found unintentionally amusing.

One such showed a couple in the act with another girl holding back a portion of anatomy to enable one to have a better view. She was wearing a fancy eye mask and was smiling into the camera with her free arm outstretched. Her stance and expression was that of a conjurer's assistant presenting the maestro's *piece de resistance*. Others showed a naked man and woman in long grass indulging in the act or gazing raptly at each other's organs. I wondered about the venue of these happenings. I'd never seen anything quite like this on Ham Common or Battersea Park – even on a hot day.

The day dragged by and it became evident that the girl was not going to arrive. The maid fed us cups of tea and swore she was expecting the girl soon and had not warned her in any way, but she was probably lying in her teeth. I had to sit on the bed as there was only one chair. I leaned back in a semi-prone position to ease my aching back. Instantly the boxer dog was upon me, a paw each side of my head and one each side of my legs, his huge wrinkled head and slobbering tongue a few inches from my face. I had heard about bestiality whilst in training school but had always been inclined to take it with a pinch of salt. I believed it now all right! The embarrassed maid yelled at the dog and dragged him off.

The photos had not shocked me but our four-legged friend certainly had.

4
Early Turn 8.30 a.m. - 4 p.m.

Another early turn patrol. At 8.30 a.m. Regent Street looks really handsome with the sun shining on the white buildings and the tarmac still glistening from its nightly ablutions. It always looks nicer when there are not many people about. The wind is sharp, though. The street seems to act like a wind-tunnel, especially at the sweeping curve by Austin Reed's.

Passers-by are brightened by the early morning sun so I am the recipient of the odd chirpy, 'Good morning, Officer', mostly from the bowler-hatted types. Believe it or not PCs are still occasionally wished, 'Good morning, Robert'!

Into the Circus.

'Nice morning,' from the newspaper seller on the corner. They always speak. We are members of the same club of 'pavement people'. A couple of minutes' chat with the PC 'on the box' (police telephone post) outside Swan and Edgar (known as the leching post because of the constant parade of interesting females) and then down to one of our hunting grounds: the tube toilets. Here in the early morning we might catch runaway girls washing and brushing up after sleeping rough or arriving from an overnight train.

But no luck today. The plump, white-coated attendant is in a talkative mood. There's no one about so I lean on the doorpost of her spotless private room while she rambles on about the dirty stove left by the previous shift. It looks pristine to me but I nod sympathetically – I might want to warm my hands here on a cold day and she's quite sweet really.

I continue up through Exit Four back into the Circus. It was here that I had an embarrassing moment recently whilst dealing with an illness in the street. A middle-aged man was coughing up blood so I called an ambulance. Someone else had the same idea. Two ambulances came racing round the Circus from different directions, screeched to a halt whereupon the man refused point-blank to go to hospital! To be fair, he had already told me he would not go. He knew what was wrong with him, had had his fill of hospitals and was not going to another one. I had been quite sure that he would change his mind when the ambulance arrived – but no.

Oh, well.

Along the front and a quick look round the amusement arcade where the attendants have a guarded, respect/hate relationship with us. Downstairs the old boy on the shooting gallery is chatty and friendly. But no pickings here so out again and along to Joe Lyons. Nice new window displays. They keep up such a good standard. Down to their marble-hall toilets garnished with aspirin and perfume machines. Not usually much for us here but it's worth a try.

Leicester Square toilets next – sometimes I feel like a lavatory inspector. Another plump toilet lady, another spotless stove. She tells me a long tale about her difficulties last night with woman vagrants and drunken prostitutes. These toms try to 'take over' the toilets and drink there whilst the vagrants just want to kip. Both are inclined to tipple on meths or similar, which doesn't help to make them tractable. And, of course, the police are never about when she needs them. Actually we have a suspicion that some attendants become too friendly with the toms and then find themselves in a tricky position when trouble starts.

Oh, there's a mate. Good, we can patrol together and chat a bit. *Verboten* really. We do have a beat each and every now and then an effort is made to make us stick to them but we soon drift back to our bad old ways. We know that it doesn't really matter very much with women police as the beat is already covered by a PC. Our type of work is mostly in defined areas which we know and anyway we operate better in twos. Officially we should only patrol together after 7 p.m.

We go through the Leicester Square gardens or, correctly, 'Leicester Fields'. How incongruous. Surprising how few people come in here. Shakespeare eyes us solemnly as we enjoy the flowers.

Let's pop down to Trafalgar Square and survey the scene. Quite a lot of girls go there to be picked up by lonely foreigners, but mainly in the evenings. We shouldn't really cross into the central part of the Square, it's not our ground and anything we get there would be 'poaching'. Still, we'll take a chance that no 'A' division coppers (monument-minders) are about.

A bus load of sightseeing Russian sailors are unloading but two remain on board.

'Those two were late back at the last stop so are being punished,' says the driver.

They look forlorn.

Through Pall Mall and into the heart of St James's. I do love this area with its elegant old shops, clubs and squares. So dignified, so eccentric and so English, as we like to see ourselves.

One morning two of us looked in the windows of that olde worlde tobacconist's over there and the equally olde worlde proprietor invited us in where he explained the finer points of snuff. We tried several different 'flavours' and were given samples. I had always thought it a disgusting habit but he made it sound most civilised and delightful.

Into Green Park. Isn't it lovely, the sun is warm on our backs but the air is still fresh. Parks are a mixed blessing to police officers. It's very pleasant to be able to stroll through them as part of a working day but we do get this persistent urge to throw ourselves down on the grass or into the nearest deck-chair. And we can't even lean on the fence. If we stop to gaze at a duck or a flower everyone in the vicinity will soon be following our gaze to see what they are missing.

It's 10.30 a.m. Time for a cuppa.

Back at the nick June has a girl in and I go and have a look in case I know her. No luck.

'Missing person inquiry for you,' says the Sergeant. That's good. Fill in nicely till lunch time.

The inquiry is at a large wholesaler's in Soho. The missing girl has a close friend there. I am to enquire if she knows the girl's whereabouts or has any ideas where she might be.

I have to pass through part of the warehouse to get to the offices.

'They've come to get you at last, Alf.' One of the workers pushes a little man forward.

'Here he is, Miss, take him away.'

I groan inwardly, Oh not again, It's as if everyone in the country has banded together and decided on a dialogue to be used when addressing police officers. But they are only being friendly and I mustn't be unkind to them.

I grin back.

'I'll collect him on the way out.'

This pleases them mightily and they all laugh and nudge Alf. I pass on quickly before the inevitable 'That's a fair cop', or 'Oh to be in the arms of the law'.

I ask the boss's permission to talk to the girl. He is hearty, friendly, and asks me questions about 'the job'. He is also very curious as 'to why I want to see Miss Jennings. It's none of his business. In fact it's confidential. But I don't want to give Miss Jennings a bad name for 'getting into trouble with the police'. I give him the rough gist of the inquiry leaving out names, etc., and making it sound as routine as possible which it is. He nods understandingly. He now feels important and in the know. A pink-faced and rather worried-looking Miss Jennings is ushered in.

'The officer would like a word with you, Ann.'

Ann nods dumbly at this unaccustomed familiarity. He settles back in his chair.

'Thank you very much, Sir,' I say with the right mixture of respect and determination.

'I'll leave you to it then,' he says jovially. 'Don't look so worried, Ann, she won't eat you.'

Heavy winks as he goes offstage.

Ann hasn't seen the girl for weeks and has no idea where she might be but will let me know if she hears anything. I thank her and leave.

'You going to take him then?' say 'the boys' on the way out, 'I wouldn't mind being arrested by you.'

I murmur some meaningless rejoinder, flash them a smile and leave on a wave of good humour muttering oaths to myself.

Most police officers talk to themselves, usually in a semi-ventriloquial manner with a stiff upper lip and through clenched teeth or out of the side of their mouths while keeping the visible side normal. If they are at very close quarters they talk to themselves without moving their mouths at all. I don't mean just thinking they actually form the words like 'stupid b____ ' (the men have a shorter favourite with more bite to it) which gives much more relief. I found this technique an essential safety valve when faced with the arrogant 'I pay your wages' or

'I have friends in high places' types or even the aforementioned well-meaning purveyors of the eternal police witticisms. On many occasions it stopped me from screaming and assisted me to smile on regardless.

Back to the nick where I phone the station which had requested the inquiry, then I fill in the enquiries book. It's lunch time.

Afternoon, and I'd like a nice quiet walk to digest lunch. One of the advantages of police work is never knowing what's going to happen next. It's also one of the disadvantages. Sometimes one doesn't want anything to happen, even if bored. One doesn't feel like coping with fresh problems.

We decide to have a walk round Mayfair. It's where I'm supposed to be anyway. Down Bond Street, casually glancing in some of the windows, longing to stop and gaze in them all. But that would look undignified. We permit ourselves the very occasional stop to look in an extra appealing window.

Outside an antique shop a small crowd is gathering. A man stops us.

'Special Branch,' he says briefly, 'I'm with the Duke and Duchess of Windsor while they're here. They're inside now looking at antiques and word seems to have got round – hence this little gathering. Will you hang on for a few minutes and keep an eye on things?'

We wait for a while. The only effect our presence has is to make a small crowd a little larger, and soon they come out – the Duke serious and haggard-looking, the Duchess elegant as always and obviously enjoying the limelight. She hesitates at the door just long enough for the crowd to drink her in. Polite clapping breaks out. The Duke looks pleased and smiles warmly, the Duchess waves graciously and smiles as they continue to their car.

'Good luck.'

'God bless.'

The gleaming limousine purrs away from the kerb.

We walk on down Bond Street, across into Grafton Street and down little Hay Hill, one of the few real gradients on the ground. Across Berkeley Street into the dinky row of shops which lead to the steps down into Curzon Street. One window always has an audience and we can't help stopping to peep at those appealing little puppies. Pedigree poodles, labradors and pekinese, they are all gorgeous fluffy balls lying on top of each other or taking a few lurching steps window-wards. The other puppy peekers grin at us. They like to see the law looking benign.

The doorman at the Washington Hotel passes the time of day. He is also in the pavement club (Mayfair branch) as are the chauffeurs who spend long hours waiting about these streets. They are usually friendly though some are a bit arrogant and feel that they should have special parking consideration naturally their biggest problem. Both doormen and chauffeurs can be the most awful snobs and some are inclined to judge people solely on the size of the tips they hand out. But not this one, he is one of our favourites.

And so into Shepherd Market to the left of Curzon Street where the afternoon prostitutes are beginning to show themselves. At our approach they make a token gesture of moving from their stationary positions and taking a very slow walk. They are beautifully dressed and coiffured and several are very good looking. There's Jennifer James a man complained about her the other day. She allegedly said to him, 'Do you want to see two naughty girls?'

He exploded, 'How dare you approach me when I have my little boy with me!'

To which Jennifer replied, 'Oh that's all right he can come and watch too.'

Up through Mount Street, the venue of the dreaded school crossing. Thank goodness I'm not on it today. Children approach the school from all directions but the largest flow comes across Mount Street so women police have a school crossing there. When it's our turn for the shift we stand here to see them into school in the morning, then out and back at lunchtime. Late turn takes the last stint. Mostly the kids come in ones and twos, as does the traffic.

This poses a problem. Do we stand there like a 'nana' holding up our hands to stop invisible traffic for one small child? We daren't let him cross on his own a car may choose that moment to roar round the corner and flatten him. The alternative is to hold the child's hand and take him across. This is OK with the smaller children but the big boys hate it and will cross farther up to dodge us. Waiting around in the winter we freeze and when one of the little dears gets a bit cheeky we feel like belting him one.

No problem, however, with a couple of sophisticated tots who arrive in a taxi and hail another after school.

One day when my beastly late turn crossing was nearly finished a lady emerged from a nearby house.

'My dear, could you stay around a little longer but not look too conspicuous? We are expecting Prince Charles to tea, a private visit you understand – no fuss. I'd just like to make sure no one bothers him. He'll be here any minute.'

She was obviously thrilled to bits and was rather sweet, so I remained and inconspicuously held off the non-existent public when Charles arrived. I think he managed the inconspicuous bit better than I did.

We cut across Grosvenor Square – Little America – and on into Oxford Street. Men with their wares spread over open suitcases on the pavement look choked as we happen on them without warning. They frantically pack up their stuff and move into the nearest doorway. Street traders in the side streets pull barrows back as we approach and pull them forward as soon as we've passed. There's that bloke with the moving snake. Amazing how it always enthralls and puzzles people. The green furry paper serpent, a few inches long slithers up and out of a tumbler then glides over his hands – apparently of its own volition. The 'mugs' fork out their half-crowns to buy. What they haven't noticed is the very fine thread joining the snake's head and the operator's jacket button. Skilful and deft hand movements and lo and behold – it snakes.

Oxford Circus. Stand outside the Spirella shop and rest our feet. The questions come thick and fast. Now and then a queue forms. Many are young foreign girls with only three words of English – 'Marks and Spencer'.

Two PCs are working the hectic Oxford Circus traffic point. A woman is poking one of them in the back as he concentrates hard on guiding lumbering buses round with little room to spare. She's fought her way out through that traffic and stopped him in the middle of his job to ask the way to Selfridges. I know because they're always doing it. If he loses his rag she'll probably complain.

An Italian comes up with a piece of paper which he thrusts into my hand. I decipher the name of a familiar street and draw a map of how to get there. It looks hideous. Still, he's pleased and seems to understand. My voice begins to get tired instead of my feet. The box flashes.

'Your Sergeant wants a WPC to come back to the nick.'

'OK, I'll come.'

The Special Branch man is in the front hall when I arrive.

'The Duke was very interested in you asked me lots of questions. He's never seen our women police before – thought you looked very smart.' Sarge says, 'The reserve's gone out with the CID. You take over.'

Just right – had enough patrolling for one day.

5
Nutters

Nutters are irresistibly attracted to police stations. Many nicks have their own regulars who pop in from time to time to pass information via police channels to MI5 or to complain about those electrical currents the neighbours will keep passing through the walls. As long as they are harmless (the nutters – not the neighbours) and able to look after themselves they impart their information, usually at great length, and then depart a little happier for having talked to someone.

The term 'nutter' was invariably used though not meant unkindly and included all types from the eccentric (a bit of a nutter) to the raving lunatic (a right nutter). The official term, 'person of unsound mind', was later superseded by 'mentally disturbed'.

As well as our chatty voluntary callers there were quite a number of less willing visitors originally brought in for criminal or semi-criminal offences but subsequently found to be of unsound mind. I remember a doctor's wife being very indignant at being apprehended merely because she had approached Oxford Circus on the wrong side of a traffic island and then pointed her car at the nearest of the two PCs on traffic duty. Disappointed by his agility in leaping out of the way, she then aimed at the second PC who, forewarned by his mate's indignant yell, also managed to execute a 'Nureyev'. But it was a close thing, Her aim was improving with practice. She was caught in a traffic hold-up further along the street by two lucky young PCs whose only injuries were to their dignity.

We did not have the power to remove persons of unsound mind from private premises. This was the job of the Duly Authorised Officer of Mental Health (this grand title was inevitably shortened to DAO) who were able to 'deem' them to be of unsound mind and detain them under a two-day order.

But the police were usually first on the scene and remained until the arrival of the DAO. As he was a very busy man this sometimes took several hours so 'waiting for the DA0' became a familiar police chore.

My first 'waiting game' was played in the huge basement packing room of a large department store. WPC Tilley (a strapping, soft-voiced girl with a delightful wry humour and an easy confidence which I envied) and I had been called there to a 'disturbance' (police parlance for anything from a minor domestic altercation to a near-riot).

We were greeted by the noise of shattering glass. A thin, middle-aged, spinster employee was roaming the basement smashing glasses and keeping all at bay with a large pair of scissors. Every now and then she let rip an ear-splitting scream. Catching sight of me she announced dramatically, 'You're a nurse!'

We tried to tempt her into a smaller side room away from the disturbing influence of the other employees who were astounded by her sudden loss of mental balance. But she wasn't going to co-operate and continued to roam so there was only one thing to do; roam with her. This we did for a couple of hours, gradually quietening her down and persuading her to relinquish the scissors. She burbled all the while about her 'Doctor' – a 'Doctor Bright' whom we eventually discovered was a small, bespectacled, inoffensive *Mr* Bright who worked in the same department. She was madly in love with him and was given to following him down the street even when in possession of her normal faculties. She was calm while we kept her talking but the moment we let up she was off on her travels round the department, snatching things from people's hands and threatening to throw a cup of coffee, which we had given her, over somebody's head.

After a couple of hours of this we were relieved (in both senses!) when the DAO arrived and we all escorted her to hospital.

On the way she announced that she was a virgin and wasn't *that* something to think about? I assured her I was in the same unfortunate position.

'I was glad I had Nurse Greenslade with me,' said Tilley kindly. 'She knew how to handle her.'

I was surprised and pleased at praise from the confident Tilley. But it was just as well that persons of unsound mind were my forte. Some officers discover a talent for catching criminals, others are dogged by sudden deaths whilst a few make a niche for themselves by summonsing everyone in sight. With me it was persons of unsound mind. I met them in the street, they came to the nick when I was on reserve duty or I was sent to them on private premises.

Not fitting into any of the previous categories was the time Mr Jones brought Mrs Jones into West End Central because he was unable to control her. They were a smartly dressed, obviously fairly well-to-do couple. Mrs Jones had been undergoing voluntary psychiatric treatment at a clinic in Central London but had suddenly decided that all the staff were conspiring against her. When her husband paid his evening visit she insisted he take her home. The cab had gone only a short way when she turned against him and refused to go further. She became so intractable that he brought her to us. He seemed very fond of her and was deeply distressed by her attitude.

Mrs Jones was a small, blonde, elegant woman with a slight mid-European accent. Though she seemed older than her twenty-five years she was quite a bit younger than her husband. She was so vehement about him I separated them straight away. I listened to her for a while then tried to persuade her to return to the hospital, but she refused.

'All the nurses hate me,' she said, 'they want rid of me.'

We decided to try to contact a particular doctor at the clinic whom she still liked and respected. Perhaps he could persuade her to return. He proved difficult to contact so I spent a long hour with Mrs Jones.

Keeping such persons happy while waiting is mentally exhausting. One must listen and enter into the conversation even if it does not make sense (they can be quick to notice an inattentive reply). One must also try to steer the conversation away from the subjects which agitate them. But most important is to keep alert from the sudden physical attack or attempt to escape. A colleague was once chatting with a very docile nutter who without any warning suddenly grabbed her by the hair and flung her across the room. Her, scalp was painful for days and a piece of bone was chipped off her ankle.

Mrs Jones was consumed with hatred for her husband.

'He wants to drive me mad,' she said, 'it was his sexual demands that made me like this in the first place. He promised to be better but as soon as I got into the cab with him he put his hands up my clothes. I will stay in a hotel in town if you will stay with me,' she decided, 'but

I'm not going to stay alone with *him*.'

I thought this was a bit too much 'above and beyond' so graciously declined.

At last the doctor phoned. He asked her to return to the hospital and she eventually agreed on condition that I accompany her. It seemed to be the best way out of a difficult problem so, with the station officer's permission, off we went in a cab. We had gone only a little way when she said, 'I've changed my mind, I want to go home. My aunt's there and she'll look after me.'

She was beginning to enjoy having us all on a string and I thought it was time I put a stop to it. I agreed to come with them (though it was way out in suburbia and much further than I had permission to go) but I made it clear that this was positively the last change of mind I would tolerate. I read the riot act and as she could not afford to alienate her last 'friend' she became contrite and behaved herself the rest of the way home.

As we reached the rather nice suburban house she said anxiously, 'You won't get out, will you? The neighbours might see you.'

Mr Jones was touchingly grateful and after paying my return fare he tentatively offered me a pound note. I gently refused and that was the last I ever saw of them. But I did hear from the Yard. They had received a gracious 'thank you letter' which had duly grown its own protective file and had been forwarded for me to 'note and report'.

Then there was the sad case of the unloved washer-up.

'Go to this ladies' club in Mayfair and sit with one of the employees until the DAO arrives,' said the station officer. 'There's a PC there already and he'll hang on if necessary.'

A pleasant, well-spoken woman showed me to the staff quarters.

'She's been with us a long time and is a very good worker but she keeps refusing to take her annual holiday. She said she had nowhere to go but we were concerned about her health and finally insisted. She was going to start her holiday tomorrow morning but asked us again if she could stay at work. When we refused she started to brood on it and then this happened.'

The washer-up was a scrawny old woman with wispy grey hair escaping from her tight bun. She was pacing her pleasant but box-like room, clad only in a vest. A young PC was keeping a watching brief from a chair just outside the door.

I persuaded her to put on some of her clothes but a few minutes later she removed them again – vest and all. The PC was obviously past embarrassment and her wrinkled old body was certainly no erotic sight, so after a few more vain attempts to dress her we left her naked. Fortunately the building was centrally heated.

She was very restless and kept leaning across her bed to open a non-existent window in the blank wall. Every now and then she made for the door saying, 'I must get down to the kitchen and do the dishes.'

This was the only time we restrained her. We couldn't get her to settle so allowed her to wander within the confines of the room. She scrabbled at the wallpaper.

'The door won't open.'

This distressed her and she turned to the bed, stripped it and pulled back the mattress revealing piles of bank notes including many fivers. She picked them up in handfuls and scattered them all over the room.

'The dishes are piling up,' she wailed and dashed again for the door. She struggled quite hard this time but it was easy to restrain her frail body.

She urinated on the floor. Some of the notes were getting soaked but she became more upset when we tried to rescue them. The chest of drawers was her next target and her few old clothes and more notes were added to the jumble on the bed.

After a couple of hours a very kindly and patient DAO arrived and she took to him straight away. I retrieved and counted all the money and handed it to the DA0 with signatures all round. We covered her up as best we could and off she went in the ambulance quite happy to leave all that washing-up behind now that she had somewhere to go.

I went to wash the urine from my hands.

6
Care or Protection

There were many reasons for instituting Care or Protection proceedings, e.g. neglect, cruelty, incest or abandonment. But our cases were mostly stereotyped due to the nature of the area we policed. There were relatively few resident children and young persons but a large floating adolescent population.

Our standard Care or Protection went something like this

A girl, or occasionally a boy, would be stopped, brought to the station and eventually found to be under seventeen years of age, to have run away from home, to be without means of support and therefore in moral danger.

But these factors alone would not justify a Care or Protection case without evidence of lack of parental control or interest. This might be shown by the fact that the parents had not reported the girl missing and/or refused to come and collect her or deposit her fare home. On occasions parents would say, 'I don't want to see her again', or sometimes the girl herself would refuse point-blank to return home. Either way we had no choice but to deal with her as 'being in need of Care or Protection'. However, if parents *were* trying to fulfil their duties but the girl would not respond and kept running away we might take her to Court. The interests of the child were the yardsticks in all cases.

The juvenile court in Chelsea which we attended was often presided over by a bench of three JPs of which Barbara Wootton (later Baroness) was frequently the chairman – and a dominant one at that. The aim of juvenile court decisions was not to punish but to assist. If possible and desirable the child or young person would be returned home and put on a Supervision Order administered by a Probation Officer. *(Probation* Orders were for offenders.) But if this was impractical a Fit Person Order might be made which handed the child over to a suitable and willing person (perhaps a relative) or to the Local Authority. The Local Authority could place them in a hostel or foster home from which they could attend school or work. Approved school orders were only used as a last resort either other methods had failed or the child or young person was quite uncontrollable or thought to be urgently in need of the facilities of an approved school.

But even so they were still not meant as places of punishment but education and assistance. The child or young person would be carefully streamed to get the right school.

All the approved schools, remand homes and even the open Borstal I visited were attractive in layout and decor. Some were lovely old houses in their own extensive grounds. The villains of the piece were the remand homes where unstreamed children (many of whom the Court would return home) were kept while they were examined and decisions as to their future made. Remands were usually for a fortnight and could be repeated. Unfortunately they exposed mildly disturbed children to far worse cases. Much thought was later given to this problem and efforts made to find better alternatives.

What happened to the juvenile after the Court's decision was not really in our province but we would have been tunnel-visioned indeed if we had never felt any concern. Too many seemed to get worse, abscond from Supervision or Fit Person Orders, land up in approved schools and continue their descent from there. Would they have got worse anyway? Did mixing with other disturbed types widen their delinquent scope? Would they in fact have been better left alone?

On courses and on visits to approved schools we often met people who were involved in this side of the work. They did not share our gloomy views and felt their success rate to be quite good. A reminder to us that we saw only the recurrent failures.

Occasionally I did feel that my action helped the situation. As in John's case.

He had left home (a caravan) because he did not get on with his mother's boy-friend who lived with them. John soon got into lay-about, thieving, homosexual-prostitute company in London and was jobless, homeless and going downhill fast.

'I'm so glad you stopped him,' his mother said, 'I didn't realise he objected so much. Fred will have to leave – John comes first.'

Mother and son were happily reunited – for the time being at least.

But after a run of such girls as 'the only virgin at the school' and 'the determined prostitute' I found myself becoming reluctant to interfere in anyone's life though perhaps this was an excuse because I disliked stopping people. Then one day I was 'stopped' in Piccadilly Circus.

'Don't you remember me? You took me to court when I ran away from home.'

She was a small, dark-haired girl, arm in arm with her smiling mum. It was eighteen months since I had seen her and I remembered her as being belligerent, anti-authority and unrepentant.

'How's everything with you?' I asked mechanically.

'Marvellous, thanks to you. I'm so glad you found me in time or else goodness knows what would have happened,' she said dramatically. Mum nodded and squeezed my hand.

'Thank you very much, we're very grateful. Everything's fine now.'

I went on my way more confused than ever.

Very occasionally we had a different type of Care or Protection involving younger children (these were usually the work of policewomen in more residential areas).

'I'm going to do a brothel,' said the Clubs Superintendent one day. 'Can I have two WPCs to take care of the three children who'll be in there?'

One imagines a brothel to be a house simply *full* of prostitutes (or whimsically a soup kitchen) complete with a madam'. But in law, two or more prostitutes working from the same premises constituted a brothel. This may seem a bit unfair but too well organised prostitution invited attendant crime. Their ponce's and protection men could get rich and powerful on the easy money.

In this case there were two regular prostitutes and an occasional third. We waited about for a suitable time to raid (or, as the newspapers would have it, 'swoop'). Evidence had been obtained on observation. The raid was merely the final move.

When one of the toms was busy with a client we 'swooped' up the rickety wooden staircase and straight into the living-room. On the bed just inside the door a tom and a client were performing. The first thing I noticed was how white and pasty the man's legs were! He jumped off and stood there looking ludicrous in his shirt tails. He was a stocky Welshman, and though a bit nervous, he seemed unmoved by what one would have imagined to be the most embarrassing moment of his life. Perhaps he was just stunned.

The room was rather scruffy and on the bedside table were packets of contraceptives, and a pair of salmon pink nylon panties. The tom was a grubby vacant blonde who smelled a bit. From the kitchen on the other side of the landing rushed another prostitute, an older woman, who was the tenant of the flat and the mother of the three children.

Big crying scenes ensued while she was told she would be charged with keeping a brothel and that the children would be dealt with as being in need of Care or Protection.

'But I've only had four men tonight,' she sobbed, 'and I put the kids to bed first.'

The logic of that reasoning escaped me.

My colleague and I went through to the bedroom where the three children were sound asleep. Two girls aged eight and nine were in bed in their underclothes whilst a four-year-old boy was in an armchair covered with a coat. To go to the toilet or get a glass of water they would have to go through the room in which Mummy and the other prostitute performed. We left them undisturbed until it was time to leave.

While we were in the flat some prospective clients came up the stairs. The first was a slim, middle-aged man.

'He's a nut,' said the older woman who was recovering her composure. 'Always goes with me first then straight after with her,' pointing to the other tom.

Two drunken soldiers staggered up the stairs. They were told that the prostitutes were not available. With courage brought on by the booze one of them said, 'I'll have her instead', pointed at me and giggled.

The chaps came over all gallant at this and threatened to break his head.

He took the hint and left.

We took the kids to a children's home and dealt with them for care or protection. They were committed to the care of the council under a Fit Person Order. The mother promised to reform if only she could have her children back after her short prison sentence, so the situation was to be reviewed then.

There *was* a father in all this – a mild-looking man who was out at his evening work when the raid took place and claimed to be completely ignorant of all the goings on. He did know that she had been a prostitute but she had promised him she had given it up! I really didn't know whether a practising prostitute mum was better than no mum at all.

I suspected she might be.

7
On Reserve

I liked reserve duty. It was a relaxing interlude. The calm could soon be shattered by frantic activity but I was on home ground with its atmosphere of camaraderie and humour. So, this was when I could drop my public face and be a person at least part of the time. Also I liked most of the work.

The main purpose of reserve duty, at which we took turns roughly once a week, was to keep a WPC available in case she was needed. Side duties were answering the telephone and keeping telex and telephone message books up to date so as to keep the patrolling WPCs informed about the latest 'wanted' women and girls likely to be in the West End. Dealing with callers at the station was also a big part of a reserve's job. The variety was endless: nutters, persons reporting relatives missing or sometimes requesting advice before instituting a personal search of the West End, and those destitute and seeking accommodation – these varied from the vagrant type to teenagers who, on further investigation, often turned out to be missing from home. There were parents unable to influence their children and wanting the police lady to have a word with them and many other non-categorical instances such as the wife who wanted her husband followed as she suspected he was being unfaithful and the husband who asked us to do something about the orgies in which his wife was taking part.

We also assisted Matron with difficult prisoners or acted as matron when she was absent. This entailed searching, staying with them while charged, locking them up if not bailed immediately, and obtaining their meals.

Searching, in most cases, was to ensure the safety of the prisoners' property (and prevent allegations against us), to inform the magistrate how much money prisoners had on them when arrested, and to remove articles with which they could injure themselves or others. But sometimes the search had a direct bearing on the charge such as in shoplifting, possession of drugs or in allegations of other recent larcenies. The most common of the latter were accusations by prostitutes' clients that the women had stolen their wallets whilst they were otherwise diverted. We rarely found the money. The man seldom missed it early enough and the girl wasted no time in getting rid of it. Although I did once find the requisite bank roll of £15 tucked into the indignantly innocent prostitute's belt.

Unhampered by the average women's fastidiousness the prostitute was liable to hide things in her vagina. This posed a problem. We would leave ourselves wide open to allegations if we investigated ourselves but to keep calling out a doctor 'just in case' would not make us very popular. Suggestions that I sometimes heard such as 'get her to jump off a table to dislodge it' merely showed a poor knowledge of female anatomy. It was a problem which tended to be ignored. The only consolation was that if they had had the opportunity to do this they would often have had the chance to pass the money on to a friend or ponce which was far more likely. It was essential to prevent unescorted visits to the toilet before searching. Rapid, unchecked flushing away of sanitary towels had also to be discouraged (we once found Indian hemp in one such item). I should imagine HM Customs have a problem there.

The previously mentioned fingerprinting and obtaining of antecedents of new prostitutes was another reserve duty. Sometimes we had a queue.

The CID or Clubs office often asked for the loan of a WPC and, if urgent, the reserve would be loaned. Most frequently we were needed to escort a prisoner or suspect or to sit with her in a waiting-room. Sometimes our detectives would ask us to have a chat with the person detained in the hope that the woman's touch would extract information where they had failed. Another loan job was sitting in a car to make the male officer less conspicuous whilst he was keeping observation. Rather like being worn as an accessory. I've sat in cars for hours in elegant Mayfair, cosmopolitan Soho and scruffy Brixton (following a ponce off the division). Once I was required just to walk down a street in Soho on the arm of an Inspector who was looking for a man wanted on warrant. Suddenly the inspector disappeared in the crowd. Not wanting to look too conspicuous I just wandered on down the street expecting him to appear again any minute. After ten minutes I went back to the nick. Another officer with us had spotted the wanted man and dashed off to arrest him and the Inspector, seeing what was happening, joined in. They had brought the man back to the nick and the Inspector had gone out again to look for me.

'Where've you been?' he asked a quarter of an hour later. 'We followed in your direction after we had arrested chummy but we couldn't find you. I thought you'd been picked up by a big dago and shipped to the Argentine.'

'No, but I got several short term propositions through hanging around.'

'How much did they offer?' he enquired with morbid interest.

'Two pounds.'

'Oh, only the average rate,' he said, unimpressed.

Once the CID asked me to accompany a soldier and themselves to a Soho flat. The soldier alleged that after having intercourse there (with the wife of a man he had met in a pub) his wallet was missing. It was a dirty flat as were the people in it and of course there was no wallet. I searched the woman at the station and as expected no money. But her dirty, white bra' was padded out (her bust was minimal) with, of all things, crumpled up toilet paper! Among the paper was a used contraceptive. I was charmed. She had the grace to blush.

One afternoon I played hostess and keeper to about a dozen well-dressed, mostly middle-aged men. They were assistants from some of the best jewellers in town and had been only too delighted to serve a charming, cultured, very elegant woman who asked to see expensive diamond brooches. Only after her departure did they find one of their best pieces missing. Eventually, after a long run, she was caught and was now standing in line in an identity parade ready to be looked over by the losers. The men were enjoying their afternoon off and, after trying to pick her out, they came back and told us all about it. Some identified her (amongst those who didn't was the man who had seen her most recently). All thought the parade very fair and were interested to know where we had acquired so many small, dark, elegant, Jewish-looking women. One of them was most impressed by the demeanour of the prisoner when he had pointed the accusing finger at her. She inclined her head graciously and smiled, 'Good afternoon', as though greeting an old acquaintance in perfectly normal circumstances. She was indeed the coolest customer I ever came across. Expensive down to her fingertips and never, for one moment, losing her aplomb.

When first brought in she had been most pained that a detective constable (not noted for his tact) had 'spoken to her like a common criminal'. His words, so she told me, were 'Right luv, let's have it. How many cons have you got?' Surely he could see she was anything but a *common* criminal.

One of my most unpleasant experiences whilst on reserve duty entailed handing over property to the relatives of persons involved in a dreadful street accident. A driver had died at the wheel of his bus which then ploughed into a queue of people standing at a bus stop near Oxford Circus. It left death and destruction in its wake. A Canadian youth escaped but his mother, father and English aunt were all killed. The following day the boy and his English relatives called at the station and I was asked to hand over the property of the deceased persons. I made it plain that I thought the production of a blood-stained trilby hat, an expensive but now completely fragmented camera and several other similar items would be not only cruel and in poor taste but quite unnecessary. The station officer was sympathetic but explained that all the items had been enumerated and signed over to us so it was essential to have signatures before we could dispose of them.

We decided to retain the more offensive items, describe them, explain they were now useless and offer to show them if they wanted to see them. But the boy was not sure about the ownership of some of the objects without seeing them and he asked about the camera. I told him it was useless. He seemed doubtful and I realised when he thought about it later he might be more doubtful. It was agreed that all items would be shown after all. I'd only drawn out the procedure and given it more emphasis. It transpired that the articles had little effect on the relatives who were in a daze after being up all night and had, since the accident, been involved in a continuous whirl of officialdom.

On another of my reserve days our Inspector said, 'Will you relieve one of the PCs guarding the prisoner in our detention room, for lunch.'

The prisoner being closely watched was Ernest Jan Fantle, the self-confessed killer of his wife's lover. He had taken a gun to the lover's luxury service flat in St James's and, after unsuccessfully pleading with him, shot him dead. For the comfort and convenience of all he was placed in the juvenile detention room with the double guard sitting right opposite him. I was interested to see what he was like and a little doubtful as to what topic of conversation one broached with a man who had just killed someone. Of course he was no different from anyone else and surprisingly cheerful. He soon put me at my ease and we chatted about food.

We women police also had to stay on a rota with the murdered man's highly nervous maid so we were to hear the details of the crime over and over. She was an eye witness and as self-confessed offenders have a habit of unconfessing once they have seen their horrified solicitors, such witnesses are precious. She was convinced she was in danger from whom I don't know and the CID wanted to make sure she didn't decamp or do anything silly while in a state of shock. So an elegant service flat was our base for several days and histrionic re-enactments of the drama our rather wearing entertainment. Eventually Fantle was sentenced to three years for manslaughter.

8
Late Turn 3.30 p.m. - 11 p.m.

It's a hot summer afternoon. I'm patrolling with Joan, an old friend who was in training school with me. George, a tall man dressed as a Roman centurion, strides past us up Regent Street. He's always wearing a different outfit. One day top hat and tails, the next an eighteenth-century get-up complete with tricorn and white stockings. Though he appears to spend most of his time striding about, head held high and eyes gazing into the distance, he actually busks quite a lot around the Palladium and evening cinema queues. He has a reputation for causing a great commotion when arrested. Once when someone told me that there was a Red Indian chief in full feathered head-dress down at Piccadilly Circus, I thought, 'Oh, it's just George again.' But I was wrong – there was a *real* Red Indian chief in full feathers on some long-awaited trip from his reservation. (Piccadilly Circus heap good but where are the animals?)

I long to be out in the country on a day like this. The heat is bouncing from the pavements, my serge skirt feels heavy, my feet feel hot and sticky. Still, we are lucky to have shirt-sleeve order. The PCs haven't yet and look as if they are about to expire.

Straight down to the Circus, stand for a few minutes surveying the scene and chatting to the PC on the box. The steps of Eros are littered with squatting tourists, arty types, bits of rubbish and old newspapers. I've only been on Eros island once in my whole service – getting there is much too dangerous to make it worth the trouble.

A hesitant Latin type gripping an alien's registration certificate appears before me, takes a deep breath and starts his rehearsed question.

'Plees where ees the Aliens–'

'Registration Office, Piccadilly Place,' I finish for him. 'Second right, first left.' I point down Piccadilly and hold up the appropriate number of fingers for each turn. He looks at me in awe. The PC who is posted here answers this particular question twenty times a day. How typical of us to place the Aliens Registration Office in an area known to, and able to be found by, all foreigners (thereby giving them confidence) and then hide it at the last minute in one of our quaint, fiendishly concealed 'Places' (just to cut them down to size). The office later moved to Holborn.

'Excuse me, ma'am, could you tell me where Liberty's is, please?' asks a deferential, middle-aged American trying to live down his countrymen's reputation for rudeness (unfairly gained through some of their servicemen, so often a country's worst ambassadors). He lifts his hat when he speaks to me and keeps it raised, his head turning underneath it as his eyes follow my hand signals. It looks comic and I am getting a choking feeling in the back of my throat.

'How many blocks, ma'am?'

'About four – but I never know how big an American block is.'

He grins at this and seizes his opportunity.

'Can my wife take a picture of us?'

'Well, I'm not allowed to pose but I don't mind talking to you, it's none of my business what your wife is doing with her camera.'

He conveys the conspiracy to Sadie and moves to my side so as to 'get us both in'. We chat about women police in his State. He is very nice. They go off happily to Liberty's in a cab.

'I was just saying to my friend how fresh and smart you both look, cool too. What a pity the men can't take their jackets off,' says one of two smart, middle-aged ladies.

People keep saying this to us. We're getting a guilt complex about the 'poor men'. Actually we feel a bit defenceless without the additional armour of our tunics, and not really very smart. Like most men we have shirt problems. Mine is a shirt shoulder line coming half-way between my neck and my natural shoulder – very smart. Fortunately this is partly covered by epaulettes.

Our duty arm bands rest precariously on our rolled-up sleeves (one whole turn above the elbow) and our skirts bulge with pocket books, whistles, maps and form 29 (to be signed by the vet if it is necessary to slaughter a horse!)

These bulges are usually fairly-well concealed by our tunic jackets. We don't carry much in our tunics; books, etc., make the lower pockets stick out and spoil the uniform line and it's practically impossible to put anything in the top pockets – especially for the well-developed WPC.

Fortunately the skirt pockets are wide and deep. At a pinch they can hold half-a-pound of tomatoes and a small lettuce.

'Haymarket!' the manner is brusque and the voice exaggerated Kensington.

'What about it, madam?'

'Where is it?' she demands impatiently.

'If you try "please" I might tell you,' I say icily – risking a big complaint.

'PLEASE, where is the Hay market?' she says, her voice heavy with sarcasm and her eyes saying, 'I pay your wages, peasant.'

'Over there on the right.' I wave vaguely, 'THANK YOU, madam!'

She stalks off. Some PCs would not bat an eyelid but just send her off in the wrong direction. Others would ignore her completely and a few indulge in a tit-for-tat, e.g.

Member of Public: 'Haymarket?'

PC (blandly): 'Piccadilly Circus.'

Member of Public: 'Haymarket!'

PC (more blandly): 'Trafalgar Square.'

But the best (and quite true) example of repartee is as follows:

Pompous Military Type: 'St James's Square!'

PC: 'Is he really? How unfortunate for his tailor.'

I'm always taken by surprise. I fight to control my temper while thinking of some suitable way to squash them without losing my job, and usually end up being quite ineffectual.

We idly amuse ourselves by guessing whether that girl is waiting for a boy-friend or her mother and if that middle-aged man is keeping an illicit appointment. We watch with concealed interest when their dates arrive. One could make a study of how people greet each other. Some of the most abandoned meetings are indulged in by middle-aged people – that must mean something.

A man walks right up to me but doesn't say anything. I open my mouth to say, 'Can I help you', but he walks away. He was just having a look.

'Excuse me, miss,' from a red-faced Yorkshireman, 'I've been having a look at these "Pros". Can't anything be done to clear the streets of them? My French friend says London is the worst city in the world.'

'Well, I'm afraid the law is rather inadequate and when we arrest them they're only fined two pounds. If you feel strongly about it why don't you write to your MP?'

'Oh, nobody would take any notice of me!' he laughs deferentially. 'But I do think "they" should do something about it,' he says firmly as he trots off, hands in pockets, to have another look.

'What bus do I get to Neasden?'

Oh Lord, I do hate questions about buses. Not being a Londoner most places far outside the West End are just names to me – Beckenham, Thornton Heath, Ponders End.

He looks at me confidently, expecting me to give the bus number immediately. This myth about all London PCs knowing all about London can be a great bind. Contrary to popular idea we don't get any special instruction on the city's lay-out, we learn the hard way, maps flying in the wind.

Together we consult my bus map. Fortunately he knows which direction to look.

Let's go before anyone else asks me about the buses. Keep on the shady side. My personal problem in this weather is trying to see the world around me. My sight is excellent but my eyes are extremely sensitive to strong light. In bright sunshine I need sunglasses but we are not allowed to wear them. Consequently I pick the shady side of the street whenever possible. When it's not I just hope that no one commits a heinous crime right under my nose. Squinting, watery eyes look so attractive too.

Tube toilets, then along 'the front' (Coventry Street). Crowds of people today – why aren't they all in the parks? Across the top of Whitcomb Street – had an amusing incident here last Sunday. As I was passing I noticed that half-way down it was completely blocked by a large crowd. I heard music and guessed that it was probably the Happy Wanderers (a good song and dance act which I've never seen right through). Sometimes we passed by the buskers pretending not to see them even if they were causing a little obstruction – but blocking the whole street was a bit much. I couldn't ignore it – might even get a complaint.

I approached unseen, my flat cap giving no warning – unlike the ominous and prominent helmet. I pushed my way through the crowd until I was in the front stalls. The performers took a few seconds to realise I was there. Startled, they stopped dancing mid-step, grabbed their instruments and ran all except one who was facing the crowd and almost in front of me.

He went on dancing automatically, not noticing that the music had stopped.

I couldn't resist hamming it. I folded my arms, slowly raised my eyebrows and began tapping my foot. The crowd held its breath looking from him to me and back again. Suddenly he realised something was wrong, looked around for his fellow performers and found he was alone. He hesitated, puzzled, but the crowd, who by now were nearly bursting, gave him no help. At last he looked behind him, saw me –and nearly jumped out of his skin.

The crowd roared with laughter whilst my poor victim looked pained (whose act *was* this?} and fled through them.

I had kept quite deadpan throughout but couldn't stop my mouth from twitching now. Quickly wending my way through the crowd who were still falling about I headed briskly up Whitcomb Street. A rather elegant young man hurried to keep up with me. He was clutching his ribs and chuckling.

'Officer,' he gasped, 'Officer, I really must congratulate you. I haven't seen anything as funny as that in years!' I felt like going back for an encore.

Into Leicester Square, the street photographers are out in force today.

'Hello Darlin's, you look gorgeous – still using Tide I see,' says one of a cheeky Jewish group. The photographers' attitude to the police is mostly friendly and cheerful and they're rarely any trouble when arrested (for obstruction). But we do know that some are over persistent and sometimes abusive to the public. Arresting them now and then prevents them becoming too much of a menace.

The 'smudge's' normal procedure is to step in front of people and 'click' his camera. This intimidates the less sophisticated or foreigners anxious to do the right thing so they stop when he speaks. After persuading them to buy 'that lovely natural shot' he insists on exposing another frame 'just to make sure'. Nine times out of ten he just pretended to take the original. He collects the money and promises to send on the photographs – a few don't.

Left up Charing Cross Road to Cambridge Circus. Into Soho via Old Compton Street. Gay and sordid Soho. Exotic delicatessens exuding spicy and cheesy smells on the warm air, the delicious aroma of fresh ground coffee, wine shops with their attractive displays of glinting bottles, the continental patisseries – windows oozing with temptations — and of course the restaurants of every type and nationality. Italian names predominate, the English are aliens here.

The afternoon toms are out. Certain prostitutes work only in the afternoons, some are housewives who have to get back to make the dinner but most in this part of Soho are the business-like continental types.

Past the '2 I's' and 'Heaven and Hell' (Hell is downstairs) coffee bars, forerunners of their type. Juke boxes, espresso coffee, guitarists (Tommy Steele and Lionel Bart started here) and lots of kids – some of them potential customers of ours.

But nothing here today.

Oh dear, there's a traffic jam at the junction of Wardour Street and Brewer Street. There are always jams in these tiny Soho streets, especially at this junction. Very few of our women police like dealing with traffic. Partly lack of knowledge, partly lack of practice and partly a complex about being women (men expect you to be bad). In addition, motorists are often too busy gaping at a policewoman doing traffic duty to take any notice of her signals

I've known only two policewomen who actually enjoyed traffic duty. One was 'Aussie' (or 'Shirl'), a typical forthright girl from down under who was always competent, whilst the other was an ex-Roedean girl who thought it was just heaven. This product of a top public school adored our hated school crossing and when finished would dash along Park Lane to beg the PC on one of the Hyde Park gates to let her 'give him a run'. Though a little doubtful at first (the points were quite complex) the PCs soon found that she was as good or better than they and thence accepted with alacrity.

She would return to the nick all chuffed having had a lovely morning: school crossing, two or three points and school crossing again. Ugh! The mere thought made the rest of us shudder. She thus became a firm favourite with arm-waving PCs. The trouble was they then began to look at us and say accusingly, 'Margaret always gives us a run – why can't you?'

She shared a passion for motor-bikes with a boy-friend who clearly adored her, plain and devoid of make-up though she was. Their romantic conversations were spiced with sparking plugs and overhead camshafts and Margaret's cup was full when he let her have a burn-up on his thousand c.c. machine – with him on the pillion.

After all, her bike was only a five hundred.

Ah, we've cleared it, more by luck than judgement perhaps but let's go before it gets bunged up again.

Through into noisy, colourful Berwick Street market. Beautiful fruit and veg. to be had here at very competitive prices. The stall holders are licensed and many have been here for years.

But those barrow boys perched on the end of the street and blocking the traffic are not. They are a different breed – younger,- sharper and often 'dodgy'. That one is selling strawberries only very cheaply. Many of them stick to one line like this and it can be a good buy provided that you want to eat the fruit straight away (they buy low-priced very ripe stock) and you watch for the tricks of the trade.

A favourite ruse has a dual purpose. During lulls between customers the fruit is picked over and the odd soft or bad pieces are removed. This keeps the display looking good. The bad fruit is then placed in the topmost of the brown paper bags (belled open – supposedly ready for the next customer) which hang on a string behind the barrow. When the customer arrives the seller tears the top bag from the string, holding it underneath with one hand and flicking it further open with the other. Quickly, he fills it with more fruit. Off goes the customer quite unaware that the fruit at the bottom of the bag is squishy or even rotten.

Another more obvious dodge is the 'no weigh' technique. The bag of fruit is on and off the scales before the weights have time to tip over.

The real market people are a cheerful, likeable lot. We pick our way through the milling crowd and over fruit wrappings, boxes and other impedimenta. The fruit looks plump, fresh and tempting. Succulent grapes, crisp shiny apples, furry golden peaches and very ugly Ugli fruit.

'Got some lovely peaches today, darlin',' says one of the hardworking stall women. That means they must be good. I can't resist for peaches are my passion. I buy one for after dinner. Joan's not interested she's an apple connoisseur.

Needless to say I get the best. Paying is often difficult. When I insist (I always do) and absently pocket my change (I always do) I may find later that I've got my half-crown back in sixpences.

Around the corner, into the Rio Grande cafe, and down the rickety curving stairs. The fresh, sunny afternoon gives way to murky, semi-darkness, deafening sexy music from the juke box, an atmosphere like a smoky Turkish bath and the smell of hot, dirty, tightly-packed bodies.

We hesitate at the bottom of the stairs whilst our eyes adjust to the light. Starting from the left we pick our way over the outstretched legs (some deliberately) of those lining the wall and around the entwined, pulsating bodies on the floor.

I feel rather ludicrous togged up in severe uniform and presenting stern authority in this sensual atmosphere. Rather like Brown Owl at an orgy.

We calmly flick our eyes over each person as we move slowly round. The reactions vary. Studied disinterest, contempt, loathing and a little insolent lechery.

All very melodramatic.

A sheepish, half-checked grin over there from a girl we know well – an old customer. Now a young man, pushing the other way, looks straight into my face from about three inches away with an expression of such fierce hatred that it actually penetrates my armour but I don't let it show. He stands defiantly in front of me blocking my way. It's him or me. This is not the place to start a punch-up. There is only one exit and that's through a thick, hostile crowd who would just love to see me go down. Then they could all put the boot in without any comebacks. But to show weakness encourages them.

'Excuse me,' I say slowly and firmly. He hesitates, realising he is at the moment of decision.

'Excuse me,' – a little louder this time with what I hope is a note of command in my voice. I move forward in a manner which suggests that I do not expect any further opposition.

His uncertainty defeats him and he moves to one side in some confusion. I push past unconcernedly but my heart is thumping and I resist the impulse to look back. Incident over.

Good heavens, there's one of our blokes all scruffy and unshaven sitting on the wall bench. Must be doing an observation. He deliberately stretches his legs out as I approach and he gives me the bored, beneath contempt look. I take care not to hesitate or register any change of expression. Good luck to him – doing a place like this. Out of the corner of my eye I can just see him making a face at our backs.

A brave young man makes as if to spit as we pass. We ignore it which spoils his fun. Right in the thick of it now, the claustrophobic effect of the heat, smoke, noise and mass of humanity in this tiny basement makes panic lurk in the back of my mind. If a fire started here!

As I squeeze through a tightly-packed corner a handsome, untidy young man brings his face close and mutters sexily, 'Yes please!' He's cheeky but his eyes are intelligent and friendly. He is really extending a sympathetic hand and conveying, 'Don't let it get you down'. I allow a slight flicker of amusement to cross my face – no one else sees. Occasionally one comes across this type in these places – unable or unwilling to conform to normal society but not fitting in here either. Too much intelligence and too little hate and resentment.

Ah, we don't know *her*. She looks very young, dirty, unkempt and similar to one of the photographs on our 'Wanted' board. She is trying to avoid our eye.

'Can I have a word with you, please?'

'What for?'

'You look like someone we are looking for.'

She looks defiant, I look determined. Grudgingly, she moves over to a small space in the crowd with me. I try to make myself heard above the din.

'What's your name?'

'How old are you?'

She answers abruptly.

'Come on outside, we'll be able to hear ourselves better.'

'No, I'm not coming and you can't make me.'

'Very well, it makes no odds to me – it'll just take longer.'

I struggle on in the deafening noise trying not to be forceful until I have reasonable grounds. But her answers are too pat and some of the details don't add up. She's lying.

'I'm not quite satisfied with your explanations. Will you come to the phone with me while I do a little checking? It's only round the corner.'

'No I won't! Who the hell do you think you are? Bleeding nosy bogies,' she shouts.

'What's the matter baby?' a huge Jamaican slightly unsteady on his feet leans over us and breathes alcohol in our faces. He is about a foot taller than me.

She tells him.

'She's telling the truth,' he says flatly as if that closed the subject, 'I can vouch for her – she's my girl-friend.'

We are used to men claiming girls we are questioning. Sometimes they are the current boy-friends but more often they do it just to thwart us and in the hope that the girl will be duly grateful.

'I'm sorry, she's coming with me.'

The Jamaican leans over a little further and looks threatening. He's dynamite. There is probably every reason for him to resent what I stand for, white authority, and he's had a few drinks. He knows he could drive me into the ground with one hand tied behind his back. But my sex and height as well as being my greatest impediment in such situations are conversely also my trump card. Not many men will hit a woman – in public anyway.

But he is not used to having his obvious physical menace ignored and it throws him. I must have some secret weapon. He looks perplexed so I jump in with the reasonable approach and explain in carefully non-patronising tones:

'I'm afraid I can't take your word for it. I still think she may be this girl so I must check on her. If she isn't she has nothing to fear. I am sure you will agree that I have no choice. It won't take long.'

I'm appealing to his reason and speaking to him like an intelligent human being and he finds the mixture irresistible. 'You can come along if you like, I don't mind.'

'Yes, I'll come with her.' He is grateful for the opportunity to give way without loss of face.

'You needn't bother, I'm not going,' she snaps.

'Oh yes you are, young lady.' I've had enough messing about. I grab her arm and start to march her across the floor. She struggles but her very high heels put her at an immediate disadvantage, one pull and she's off balance. This is too much of an indignity.

'All right, all right, I'll come,' she whines, pushing my hand away petulantly. I let go.'

'Right, come on then.'

Our posse moves out. We make the blessed sunlight. Joan is there already with a girl she has stopped.

'Pity you can't close that awful place round the corner, dear,' mutters one of the stall holders as we pass. 'Don't be daft – we'd be redundant.'

They all laugh at this. A welcome sound.

We troop over to Trenchard House (the men's section house) which is a couple of minutes away. A CID aide comes alongside.

'OK luv?' he enquires, glancing meaningfully at man mountain.

'Yes thanks, no trouble,' I smile.

He's reassured and drops behind but follows us discreetly until we reach the safety of Trenchard. The men fuss over us like hens over day-old chicks.

Joan has caught us up, her girl was OK. She stays with mine while I phone. Policemen of all ranks and modes of dress mill up and down the entrance stairs and in and out of the canteen. They scan our companions with mild interest (they are used to their home being used as a police station).

'Bully.'

'Is that the only way you can get a man?' and such like remarks are muttered in my ear while I telephone.

I tell Index the name Joan Wright, age 18 years – date of birth and approximate height, five feet four. They are gone for a while.

'Nothing under the name. There are a couple of absconders who've only been out a few hours. One's five feet four, wearing jeans and black sweater, has brown hair, blue eyes, long face – she's seventeen.'

Height and jeans tie up all right but ours is wearing a red sweater, has a round face and looks younger than seventeen. She looks as if she's been sleeping rough so it's unlikely that she's just got out. Still, she's a possible.

'Nothing about accent?'

'No.'

'Anything else?'

'I'll just go and look in the birthday index... Yes, we've got something here. A girl with the same day and month.' (Girls often change the year but seem to stick to their day and month.)

'Her name's Jean Richards, fifteen years, missing from home in Leeds since a week ago. Five feet six, blue eyes, red hair, oval face; slim build, wearing blue coat, grey dress, black shoes. Bites fingernails.'

'That sounds a bit more like it. The hair and age tally better and she's slim. But she says she's from West Hartlepool and her accent's certainly more Geordie than Yorkshire. Hang on, I'll have a look at her nails.'

She is reluctant to show them to me. I notice that her Jamaican friend has drifted away – the sight of so many policemen I expect.

'Yes, she bites them. Also got a scar on her left hand – anything about that?'

'No.'

'Right, thanks for your help. I'll let you know what happens.'

I go back to the girl and try the name Jean Richards on her but she is unmoved. Mmm – I meditate – decision time again. Description fits but only vaguely. On the other hand she's dodgy enough in her own right: looks young, has been sleeping rough and is dirty and smelly. I take the plunge.

'I'm not satisfied, I'd like you to come to the station for a further check.'

She takes it surprisingly calmly.

'You've already checked on me. Pity you've got nothing better to do.'

At the station I phone the West Hartlepool Police and ask them to do a home check. Then I go over her story with her again. She's eighteen, comes from West Hartlepool, has been in London about a year and has worked as a hostess at various clubs.

I try to trip her up with questions but she's too adept. Less cocky now but just as determined.

Back to the office where I scan the pictures on the board, so tiny and many of the faces surprisingly alike. The one I thought she might be has gone, that girl's been caught.

'That could be her. Take away the long hair and glasses,' says the reserve WPC helpfully, pointing at a Borstal escapee's photograph.

'Let's see no, it says "eyes brown" – they are usually right.'

All the girls coming in for dinner have a look at her in case they have seen her before. No luck. I find a PC from Durham who knows West Hartlepool well and he talks to her.

'She knows the town all right,' he shrugs.

I wade through police publications checking lists and descriptions of missing and wanted girls. Often useful but these can also be confusing she could be any one of a dozen.

Oh well, nothing more we can do until we hear from West Hartlepool.

I take her some tea and a bun which she scoffs ravenously, then I leave her alone while I have my dinner. The lull often does the trick.

'That's a nice peach,' says Sergeant Bush suspiciously.

'Yes, we have a good greengrocer near the section house,' (true). But she doesn't press it. The Sarge is all right. A bit terse when she's got one of her headaches said to be the result of a coshing she received when playing a decoy to a habitual sexual assaulter in Croydon. She holds the George Medal for that – perhaps two or three aspirins are of more use.

Half-way through my peach and West Hartlepool ring back. That's quick – it often takes a couple of hours or more.

'Street exists all right and the number but she's not known there.'

'Ta very much, that's just what I wanted.'

This sort of reply always makes us feel better. At least we know that the girl is lying and can presume she has some good reason. Back to the room where I find she's nodded off to sleep. I wake her.

'Nobody knows you at the address you gave – and don't give me the bit about the wrong number.'

She opens her mouth to speak but can't marshal anything good enough so closes it again. She's at low ebb.

'We think you're Jean Richards. We're going to get your mother to come down.'

'She won't come, she doesn't care about me.'

I show no surprise at the roundabout confession though I feel some relief and the satisfaction of being right. 'She cares enough to report you missing.'

We get the lot then. Parents don't understand her, Leeds is dead (she had lived in West Hartlepool before hence the accent and knowledge) and she'd had a great big row with Mum who doesn't like her enjoying herself. (Reunion next day was tearful and affectionate on both sides.)

I point out the alternative to returning home – Care or Protection and that she'd be better off with Mum until she was a bit older and could then come to London with a job to go to and somewhere to live. Also that she should try to see Mum's point of view. OK, she'll give it a try. That's all right with us as it's the first time she has run away and she was reported missing.

Parents are sent for. Answer comes back that they will collect in the morning. I complete a pocket book report, make an entry in the 'stop book' and give details to the station officer. I will send written reports to the Yard and West Hartlepool police tomorrow. The reserve can get Jean a proper meal now that she is 'official'. I was lucky, I got a lead on this one straight away which made it fairly quick and easy.

It's half past nine, out on patrol again. Rio Grande cafe, another stop but she's all right. On to the Ding Dong club, same style as the Rio Grande but larger and isolated at the top of several flights of stairs.

As we leave the Ding Dong we bump into the Angel. He's tall, rangy, with skin-tight pants, long dark hair and plum-coloured lipstick.

'Darlings!' he cries, 'I haven't seen any of you for ages. I've been wanting to ask your advice. This little bitch took my suitcase and...' We listen to his tale of woe. He is rather amusing and loves having girl-to-girl chats with women police. Once when arrested he begged a pencil and paper and whiled away his time in the cell sketching fashions and exhorting the wary PC gaoler to 'Come here darling and let me draw you'. This type of homosexual often finds policemen attractive – the job has such masculine overtones. Another of the more wildly exhibitionist types who was a habitual drunk always begged to have his charge dealt with by 'that lovely, big, brutal-looking Sergeant!'

We make our way through the back-doubles towards Piccadilly Circus. The toms who literally line some of the streets move lazily and automatically as we approach. With the great upsurge of interest in the problem of vice on the streets there are additions to the usual 'tom-watchers' (men who get a kick out of just standing hands in pockets – some surreptitiously masturbating – looking at the girls, sometimes for hours). More professional observers, journalists, 'up Westers' and tourists than usual because newspaper publicity has made prostitutes and relatively powerless police one of the accepted sights. (Though, to be fair, it also led to a change in the law soon after.)

We cross the brilliance and bustle of the Circus into Regent Street. That's late turn over till tomorrow unless something crops up on the way to the nick.

Shortly after this we were ordered to take a PC with us when visiting the Rio Grande, Ding Dong and suchlike dens of iniquity. We were very cross – the inconvenience of looking for a PC, then having him stand there attracting even more attention, we found very irksome.

The implication that we were incapable of looking after ourselves was a bit much as well.

I buttonholed the PC we had seen undercover in the Rio Grande.

'I hear that it's *your* fault we have to take a PC with us.' He grinned, unrepentant.

'And about time too!' he said with feeling. My heart used to hit my boots every time I saw you girls come down those stairs. Don't you realise how dodgy it is? They have knives, knuckle-dusters, sometimes even guns. They're hopped up with drink or drugs and they hate your guts. I couldn't have done much if you'd got in a fix – everyone would have put the boot in. I've heard them talk about what they'd like to do to you.'

'I've even seen some of you girls come down there alone! Alone!' The thought obviously gave him sleepless nights.

'We realise it's a bit dangerous but we think you've exaggerated. Anyway, none of us has been beaten up yet.' He sighed and shook his head in mock despair.

'You sound like the motorist who's been driving like a maniac for years and boasts that he's never had an accident!'

9
Standing on Ceremony

As usual we are on the spot hours before the event is due to start. A few early birds are already staking their claims to the better view points and more are slowly drifting in. There is a nip in the air but the early sun is bright in a cloudless sky. Looks as if it might stay that way. The nearest toilets and lost children posts are vital information in our pocket books. Even more important – the whereabouts of the police refreshment tent. Not that one could miss its huge, grey shape squatting in St James's Park.

The PCs in their quaint, high-buttoned 'number one' uniforms look as though they have stepped out of a faded print with horse buses and ladies in long dresses. The close-fitting jackets have the effect of making portly peelers look portlier and tall, thin jims look positively tubular. Awfully hot for summer wear but I am told that the high neck is partially compensated for by the fact that one doesn't need to wear a collar and tie. A vest underneath is often sufficient. We too get instructions to wear our 'number ones' but as these are exactly the same as our 'number twos' (two jackets and three skirts are issued one set kept as best) a bit more 'bull' is the only difference in our appearance.

The voluntary ambulances and their eager attendants are arriving and line the rear of the Mall. Not much to do yet so I chat, reply to questions from foreign visitors (most of whom don't listen to the answers – they just want to add talking to a 'lady bobby' to their London experiences) and wonder who decided that the tarmac in the Mall should be deliciously different – pink in fact.

English mums strike up conversations with us when possible. There's a carnival atmosphere and they must show these numerous foreigners that this is 'our' do and illustrate that our police are much more approachable than theirs.

Hallo, there's Colin Sanders. Haven't seen him for months, he must have transferred.

'Haven't seen you for ages, Where are you now?'

This is the play safe question when one can't remember if or to where they transferred.

'Still on "Z" Division.'

"Z"?' I look suitably disdainful. 'Where's that? I know, it's somewhere in the sticks.'

But he's used to 'sheep dip' cracks by now.

'Arr, they be lettin' us cum to the big city today,' he grins.

All ceremonial events and big demonstrations are occasions for cops' reunions. Many young men start their service on inner divisions and move out when they buy a house or go in for promotion. They quite enjoy a day 'on loan' to their old stamping grounds.

Oh, the lovely guards are coming to line the route. Cameras click as the troop marches stiffly down the Mall fanning off at intervals until the whole road is fringed with scarlet. The crowd grumbles about the added restriction to their view. A plump, pink-cheeked officer approaches 'our' guardsman and gives him unintelligible orders. He shuffles to square up with his mates.

'Get him,' derides a middle-aged mum indicating the officer, 'thinks he's the cat's pyjamas!'

One or two more PCs filter into the line-up. I move along to let one in and my people object strongly. He's tall, I'm small.

'We don't want him, he's too big. Won't see a bleeding thing behind.'

He blushes and tries to fit in elsewhere but gets the same reaction. He decides to remain and ignore the objections — not much choice really.

The sun is blazing down now — those poor guardsmen.

Getting near time. Some kids are still at the back. I pull them to the front and no one has the nerve to object.

Interspersed with bands, the guards who will take part in the actual ceremony march smartly up the Mall.

'Who's he then, an admiral or something?' asks the middle-aged mum as an equestrian in a navy, frogged uniform and a tricorn hat hoves uncertainly into view.

'Don't look very safe on that horse, does he?'

I grin to myself. I know who he is. He's one of us. It's a treat for police officers on these occasions to see their very superior officers, e.g. Assistant Commissioners or Commanders, so obviously ill at ease in their musical comedy get-ups and mounted on very tame but very large horses. Some PCs may find their superiors' lack of dignity embarrassing but console themselves that no one else knows who they are.

Open carriages now with some of the Royal family and guests. As they get closer cameras are thrust out as far as possible and I keep my eyes open for the opportunist who may dash into the road to take an approach shot.

One of our Australian WPCs tackled this photographic problem in the best manner. She filmed the full dress rehearsal which is far less crowded and then on the actual day concentrated entirely on getting good shots of the Queen and any celebrities present.

Here comes the Royal procession at last.

A gleaming of breast plates as the Household Cavalry draws nearer. Aren't they picture book magnificent? An interval and then their mounted band followed by the Sovereign's escort and the Queen riding slightly ahead of Prince Philip. She looks tiny, immaculate and worried. He looks dishy and as masculine as ever.

They are followed by lots of important-looking mounted guards (including Gold-stick-in-waiting and the inferior Silver-stick-in-waiting).

They are past.

I answer the twentieth question about the nearest loo, cup of tea and 'when will they be coming back?' then go for my cuppa in the big top. The smell inside reminds me of my misguided attempts at camping with the Girl Guides but I'm glad to be inside – the heat out there is getting unbearable. I reflect that I've been on several Troopings of the Colour but have never seen the actual ceremony. I always get the Mall.

As the day has stayed so fine there is a much larger crowd forming for the return. They gather early and then get impatient, the wait seems interminable.

The Household Cavalry come trotting down the Mall from Horse Guards Parade. I gaze in awe at the shiny, be-plumed soldiers riding to attention, eyes straight ahead. But nevertheless one of them catches my adoring eye, slowly lowers his right eyelid and is gone. No one saw but me.

Ah, at last 'they' are coming.

Everybody leans forward to get first glimpse in the distance – there have been several false alarms. But this time it is 'they'. The Queen and Duke first, followed by the noise and colour of the massed bands and scarlet-coated guards whose colour has been trooped. Everyone 'oohs' and 'ahs'. That bearskin the Duke is wearing isn't quite him, is it?

But every eye is focused on the Queen, a pale, serious figure. Clapping and spasmodic cheering break out. More and more people start to run along the back of the crowd so as to stay alongside, their eyes on her all the time seemingly hypnotised.

'It's jammed, it's goddam jammed!' exclaims an American voice almost tearfully.

They're past.

'How do you like that?' he says disgustedly. 'Just as those guys came into view it jammed, it jammed!'

He looks at the offending camera with loathing.

We have been instructed to keep the crowd from the middle of the road until the guards lining the route have been marched away. A none too rapid procedure. The crowd thinks that we are indulging our power complex. But for the guards to group and then march through jostling people would be undignified if not impossible so we weather a few objectionable remarks from the 'I-have-my-rights' brigade and stick to our guns as far as possible.

As the crowd drifts away the whole area is seen to be covered with litter. Before Princess Margaret's wedding a special anti-litter appeal was made. The crowd responded with the worst littering I have ever seen, literally knee-deep in places.

Oh well, it didn't rain. Everything went off well and it didn't rain.

State Visit

The Royal Air Force are lining the route along Whitehall and the Mall. Well aware of the honour, they've made the plain uniforms look as snazzy as possible with whiter-than-white hat-bands, belts and gaiters.

Oh dear, it's starting to rain. 'They' are not due for quite a while and there are few spectators. I'll retreat into a doorway. The rain is increasing to a steady downpour. It soaks into the Air Force blue with scarcely a trace at first.

Now it's torrential, bouncing off the pavements and just goes on and on. The uniforms begin to darken as they become more and more saturated.

Oh no! The white is starting to run. The final ignominy. Soaked to the skin and now all that 'bull' going down the drain literally. The blanco streaks on to their faces, down their tunics and even drips on to those mirror-like boots.

Curses on our weather.

It's slackening a bit now and 'they' are due. I'd better go out to the edge of the pavement. I'll stand next to one of those poor airmen. Damn, it's belting down again. A young lady has appeared behind us, she has a large umbrella which just happens to cover the three of us. She gazes down Whitehall not noticing our existence. I of course do not realise that I am being protected from the downpour and what can the airman do?

The short procession of gilded carriages draws opposite, the good Samaritan judiciously withdraws the umbrella, the rain stops and the sun breaks through the clouds. Would you credit it!

Premiere

Big do this time a Royal Film Performance. Crowds throng two sides of Leicester Square. I am in the line-up outside the cinema foyer.

The lesser guests are arriving in dribs and draw. A Council road sweeper tidies up after one of the two police horses and is cheered by the crowd for his pains.

'That's a gorgeous dress, David,' says one of the right ravers behind me.

'But not with those shoes, dear,' says David disapprovingly.

What a pity the backs of the dresses get so creased up in the cars, think I. The poorer, early arrivals fight a battle with the 'what to wear over the dress so as not to crush it, keep warm, look nice on arrival and not break the bank for one occasion' problem. They all lose.

A huge gleaming black car flaunts itself among the taxis and minis. A rich-looking dress followed by a richer-looking fat man alight. Ah, this must be somebody. Everyone strains to get a look at her face and are disgusted when they don't recognise her. She's nobody.

'Who are you then, darling?' shouts David.

Evidently the Press think they *are* somebody. When they make the shelter of the foyer a few flash bulbs pop (I get a sneaking feeling that they pop for anyone who looks important – just in case).

The pace is hotting up a bit now and the traffic chaos worsening. Most of these affairs must take place without stopping the usual traffic flow and naturally the West End cinemas are on busy streets. The ultimate nightmare is the London Pavilion right on Piccadilly Circus (though more recently in a moment of wild bravado it was decided to hold a Beatles premiere there).

More recognisable people now, character actors (those familiar nameless faces) and one or two stars. There's Brigitte Bardot, she looks pale and nondescript in a colourless gown. Obviously trying to look 'proper' for Queen meeting. Arlene Dahl, cool and demure in navy net with a cream satin top. Then Ian Carmichael, Dana Andrews and Belinda Lee.

Our bevy of braid which appears en masse at these Royal affairs is starting to mess up the traffic. They congregate in bunches in the road and outside the cinema. When a couple of cars draw up to unload simultaneously they feel they ought to be doing *something* so start waving their arms frantically, much to the confusion of the car drivers who don't know which one to obey in addition to being intimidated by all that scrambled egg on their caps.

'Swirling the bath water again I see,' says a PC next to me who could do the job better with his eyes closed.

Thick and fast now. Marilyn Monroe, snowy bosom spilling out of her tight, gold lame dress and looking up appealingly at her husband Arthur Miller for reassurance. Anthony Steele with wife Anita Ekberg surprisingly clothed to ankle and wrist in high throated, demure white lace. But it fits like a first skin and shows an astonishing profile of her huge breasts uplifted and each one going its own way – outwards.

'Ch—rist!' exclaims a male voice behind me as she passes. Most well-known people are a bit of a disappointment when seen, mainly because they look like ordinary humans. Reasonable enough I suppose. Both sexes appear smaller than imagined (for me the exception was Sophia Loren in a long column of a gown with matching coat; when waving she raised her arm straight above her head which made her look gigantic). Faces too are smaller. Features we have seen feet-high in close-up, more insignificant.

Joan Crawford (another high waver), elegant in cream satin, wins the approval of David's friend. David is reservedly impressed.

The bath water is being swirled with a vengeance now. The

appointed time is nigh and the front must be clear for 'her'. The Council representative gives a final sweeping and the red carpet goes down. Cheers all round.

'This Royalty business is a lot of hooey,' comments a young American serviceman to his English girl-friend.

'Oh, she's nice,' says the girl defensively.

But he keeps up a barrage of mickey taking.

They are late. The odd, last minute car is frantically hustled out of the way barely allowing the passengers time to alight. We wait and wait and wait...

Now they are coming, eyes strain to catch the glint of the approaching black car. As it draws alongside, the American catches his breath.

'It's fantastic – she's like a fairy princess!'

And indeed she is. No Royalist I, but I do like to see something well managed and this can't be topped. The Royal cars always shine like no other cars I have ever seen. The interior lighting is well-placed and flattering to her complexion and those diamonds.

Those diamonds! On her head the diamond and emerald tiara, a fortune's worth of solid sparkle. Her necklace and earrings glitter against the background of her black velvet dress.

How does she get away with it? That lot would swamp many a woman and indeed often looks a bit much in photographs. But here in the lights and the glamorous atmosphere it looks magnificent. I suppose that the fact they are all real helps!

She smiles and completes the picture. Everyone cheers. 'You look gorgeous, darling!' cries David, quite overcome. Margaret follows, looking pretty in pink brocade. They both smile and wave at the crowd before disappearing into the crowded foyer.

'Wasn't she lovely much nicer than her photos.'

'Ever so tiny, I never thought she was so little – Margaret too.'

After a decent interval we are told, 'O.K. Break now. Back at ten to see them out.'

And chaotic that will be I think to myself. After 'they' have left there begins the mad scramble for cars. When the car is there the celebrity isn't. When the celebrity arrives the car is no longer there – it has been waved on out of the way by irritable policemen and is being driven round the block by a furious chauffeur. Tempers become brittle, chauffeurs swear and some of the guests throw their precious dignity to the winds

and actually *walk* away!
    Another premiere is over.

10
Private Lives

The high complement of WPCs at West End Central was unique in London and probably throughout the whole country. The number fluctuated but was usually around twenty. Two were on night duty and the remainder were divided into two reliefs who worked early and late shifts on alternate weeks. The strength was frequently depleted by clubs jobs, escorts, juvenile court duties, sickness, holidays, etc.

But the most serious – and permanent depletion was through marriage. The rate of loss was tremendous but what can one expect putting twenty young women among six hundred young men?

Of the twenty perhaps half would be either married already or engaged or going steady. Two or three would be the confirmed spinster type. That usually left about half a dozen eligible girls. If a girl was reasonably attractive she would be overwhelmed with invitations. Very good for the morale. And unlike most police stations the great majority of the men were single. Married men often moved out to the suburbs to buy houses so that the West End got a continuous flow of new, young PCs.

I had my turn at playing the field but soon fell madly in love with a CID aide. I thought him the most handsome, elegant, debonair, charming and witty person I had ever met. Naturally, he wasn't *quite* so impressed with me but he eventually hove to and my life was complete.

Now for the delight of getting to know him really well and to discover our mutual interests. You've guessed it – there weren't any. It was all surface. What an anti-climax after all that effort.

But another young man who had made tentative – no blatant – attempts to win my attention away from my hero now came into the picture. He was tall, dark, quite handsome and loaded with charm. A little too much for my dour, suspicious Northern mind to appreciate

– obviously too sweet to be wholesome. I was wary but needlessly so. He was one of those men we women are always looking for – intelligent, kind and thoughtful without being staid and dull. In fact great fun to be with. My room-mate had a strong crush on him before I even knew him and she thought I was most unappreciative of my luck.

He and I were on the same wavelength immediately and after the first couple of dates we saw each other constantly. I was a little perturbed when he asked me to come home and meet his mother after only the second date. Rushing it a bit I thought (at that time any girl could confirm that men could be just as over-keen to marry as women were accused of being). But I needn't have worried, there was nothing rash about Bob. We married after two years of courtship as I was just beginning my fourth year in the police service.

It transpired that I was married in the eyes of God, the Registrar and the Inland Revenue but *not* the Metropolitan Police. How could I be? It had not yet 'come out' in Orders and I had not received my new warrant card. So for several weeks I was still Joan Greenslade, WPC 302'C' and had to sign all police correspondence thus. This made the task of adjusting to a new name and signature even more confusing. Using my new signature off-duty and my old one on-duty made me positively schizo and probably did me some permanent psychological harm. Small wonder that even two years later I still had the occasional relapse – which in certain situations could cause some embarrassment at least!

Of course having a fiancé and then for a few months a husband at the same station did have its amusing moments. One day a colleague and I saw a parked van impeding the passage of a taxi in a street approaching the nick. I went to get the van driver. As I did a man popped his head out from the taxi.

'Do hurry and get this cleared, Officer. It really shouldn't be allowed.' It was Bob, sharing the cab with another Officer and the two street photographers they had arrested. They were all in a high good humour.

Later Bob told me that as we had approached them one of the photographers said, 'That's the one I fancy – that little one.'

While his mate fell about Bob pointedly contemplated his signet ring my 'exchange' engagement gift.

'Oh re—a—lly,' he said in a slow menacing voice, 'you fancy my fiancée, do you?'

He's a terrible ham and enjoyed every minute of the spluttering gulping reaction.

We were all at the same court the following morning.

'Here, it's a good thing I didn't say anything uncomplimentary about you, isn't it?' asked the photographer. Then aside, 'Do you really like him? He's a bit thin, isn't he?'

He was a bit disappointed that I was not going to succumb to his obviously superior charms even though he had declared his interest. But he soon brightened.

'I know, I'll take your wedding pictures for you. Don't forget.'

After all, business is business.

Another time I was talking to Bob in Bond Street when a young American stopped to ask me a question and then began to chat me up. For the fun of it I encouraged him a little.

'Where are you going tonight?' he enquired.

'Out,' said Bob slowly and deliberately, 'with *me.*'

For the first time he took in Bob's six feet plus helmet and decided to abandon efforts to establish an Anglo-American special relationship.

Whilst single I lived in Pembridge, an all-female section house at Notting Hill Gate. It was a combination of three large old houses joined together by passages which gave it a rather odd lay-out but far more character than some of the modern section houses. I had lived in one of these (Tooting) for several months early on in my service. It had comfortable, convenient but identical egg-box rooms, almost exact replicas of rooms I had experienced in Nurses' Homes. In Pembridge, however, one had the choice of the privacy of a small single room or sharing a larger more spacious one, often with a balcony.

All the rooms were different. I tried sharing initially and was lucky to get one of the best rooms in the place. I had four different roommates during my stay. Two got married, one transferred and one outstayed me. I loved my balcony which overlooked a leafy square.

I also loved the service.

All cleaning was done for us, we only had to make our beds. But my cleaner always did mine in addition to making sure that I was up and out for work on time, bringing me dressing table covers, ornaments, chair covers and cushions – 'makes it look more homely'. She never actually *gave* me an object they just appeared, and later disappeared for washing!

We had a better than average canteen in one of the basements but there were also plenty of cooking facilities for those that way inclined — a room full of gas stoves in fact.

Amenities for guests were also unique. We had one huge sitting-room where we could entertain guests or have them wait for us (female guests could come to our rooms), a large dining-room opposite where we could serve food to them and last, but by no means least, the 'Little Room'. This had to be booked ahead and one was only allowed a certain number of bookings within a given time. It was small, cosily furnished and strictly private. The latter becomes a luxury to those who live and work among hordes of people.

I liked Pembridge, the attractive view and the interesting polyglot area (my own home had been situated in a replica of Coronation Street and Nurses' Homes were not half so comfortable and flexible). I even liked the fact that it was all-female which made the atmosphere more relaxed.

But about half of the West End Central girls lived in a modern section house at Putney which they declared much better than our rotten old virgins' retreat. Each to his own.

One big disadvantage of the area was that whilst very handy for the West End it was on the fringe of the prostitute belt. This meant that we had to endure a tiresome amount of being accosted especially when coming off late turn duty alone.

The worst spot was the bus stop in Bayswater Road. When we alighted we would wait for a gap in the traffic so as to cross the road and we were then invariably, and often persistently, accosted from cars. Sometimes it was worth the irritation just to see the expression on the man's face when I silently drew out my warrant card. Occasionally they would not bother to read it but go on with their chat. A curt, 'Read it!' then, 'Now beat it!' usually had them crashing their gears and disappearing into the distance. If I was feeling vindictive I would say ominously, 'I've got your car number. You realise you can be prosecuted for this sort of thing?'

Sport and hobby facilities in the Met. were tremendous. There were teams for everything from chess to water polo and endless clubs from photographic to toxophilic. That many of them flourished was due no doubt to the considerable mixture of types (misfits?) to be found in a police station.

West End Central had experts on just about everything. Magic (a

PC was a member of the Magic Circle), bricklaying, trawling, show jumping, religion and a number of officers even studied law in their spare time.

I am neither sporting nor a 'joiner' and only became part of the Women Police Choir because I felt I would let the side down if I did not do something. The other girls dashed around playing hockey, netball, tennis and even cricket. One particular girl who did all of these things better than everybody else rather annoyingly turned out to be also the prettiest and consequently the most sought after by the males.

Our Australian contingent (at one point we had three in Pembridge) were of course revoltingly active and made me feel like a big, unhealthy slug. I steadfastly refused to join the First Aid team which was the passion of one of our sergeants, though I did consent occasionally to being got up as an injured person. Lying around and being lifted about was more in my line.

I also demurred at joining that masochistic team, the Nijmegen Marchers. I was fast getting a reputation for being an unsporting non-sportswoman so although I can't sing I joined the choir. This did have the advantage of being my Inspector's ruling passion.

I can now boast of having sung at the Royal Festival Hall (rather badly) and at several Darby and Joan clubs (very badly).

The deafness of the latter's members was a great aid to their appreciation. They were just pleased that someone had come to see them.

At work we girls got on well with surprisingly little bitchiness. Although a few male officers disliked the whole idea of women police and in our training period we were dourly warned that we would be treated 'just like the men' it worked out in practice that we were generally treated like bone china. In no job before or since, and I've had a few, have I found such *esprit de corps* and humour, though I'm told that morale has since dropped as the result of the continuous public onslaught. This was alleviated somewhat by the tragic death of three policemen shot in the line of duty But intelligent police officers are not over-impressed by suddenly becoming the 'good guys' just because people are shooting them through the head. They know by experience that this can just as soon swing the other way and as one of them said, 'I'll be more impressed when they start coming to the aid of a copper who is having his head kicked in.' He'd have a long time to wait.

There was a lot of nonsense talked about police officers being socially ostracised and being forced to find their friends amongst other police officers. In fact, it was often a social asset to be a police officer, everyone wanted to talk to them. It could also be the hell of a bore. The reason they often finds friends among their own kind is that too many people refuse to forget that they are police officers. They always feel representative and it's a bit wearing when trying to relax at a party having to listen to how their fellow guests came in contact with police. The officer was wrong/rude/inefficient/stupid whilst they were right/polite/wise and finally put him in his place. Then there was the demand that they atone for a PC in the Outer Hebrides who hit a prisoner last Ash Wednesday. Or even the brain freezing, 'Have you ever caught a burglar?'

But worst of all are the endless police quips. Well-meant, hearty, self-conscious and always old. Women police had the additional burden of their curiosity or oddity value and friends would use us quite ruthlessly in this manner.

Some aspects of this sort of talk interested me. I realised that:

(A) People were not going to accept anything which did not match up with their pre-conceived ideas and prejudices, even if I talked until I was blue in the face.

(B) That for some odd reason they almost wanted it to be true that all police were violent and corrupt. Just as they insisted that I was some sort of saint when employed as a nurse.

(C) It's the idea of *Power* that fascinates them.

(D) They harboured the impression that police make laws as well as enforce them.

Fortunately most people eventually tired of this sort of thing and began to accept them as a person so that as one got older and friendships more settled these irritations lessened.

Shopkeepers who recognised the blue shirt and black tie under the jacket of the homeward bound PC would often fuss him, give him the best produce and attention quite voluntarily. Cynics will say that this is self-protection but it still happened when the trader knew that the officer policed a different area and there was therefore no point in attempting to influence or 'sweeten' him.

No, the police officer was lionised, not ostracized, but for odd love/hate/power-fascinated reasons. I know that at first I quite liked the fuss but by the end of my service I couldn't wait to be free of the burden, boredom and responsibility of, 'This is Joan, she's a lady policeman.'

11
La Dolce Vita

'How lucky you are to be paid to enjoy yourself,' friends would remark on learning that I was engaged on clubs work. In fact, I usually found the job unutterably boring. This was mainly because I was neither able to choose my company nor leave when I became fed-up or tired. My male escorts were employed on clubs work not for their social attributes but because they were keen (sometimes too keen) and they did not look like the public's idea of a police officer.

Not looking like a police officer was mainly a matter of height. Although five feet eight inches (then the minimum requirement for males in the Metropolitan Police) is fairly small, men with certain types of build can look even smaller. The general non-police image could be helped along with a few tricks. Nothing complex was necessary. For example: Long hair (policemen had short hair), a pair of plain-lens spectacles ('proper' policemen didn't wear glasses), 'way out' clothes (policemen wore fawn belted raincoats). Their own accent could also be a good disguise. 'Public school' (coppers are common), and Commonwealth (Bobbies are British) were both very effective.

One dashing Australian PC who dressed like an American was out on clubs almost before his feet had time to measure a beat. They grabbed him with glee as soon as he hit the division and he was a roaring success.

Short men need short companions and that was where I came in. At five feet four and three-quarters I was short by women police standards (we had a couple of six-footers at West End Central).

Sometimes I went along for all the observations at a club and sometimes just for one or two. Once I did the final hour on the raid evening. Two male officers felt that they were looking conspicuous without a woman companion and were afraid the job might 'blow'. One of them phoned the nick, I was taken off the waiting raid party and rushed in to join them for a dance or two.

My first clubs job was on another division. I was loaned out to partner a Sergeant who was also on loan from elsewhere. He looked so unlike the 'public's police officer' that when he had occasion to declare himself no one would believe him! Twice in fact members of the public had rung the local nick to report him for impersonating a police officer.

We were taken by the Superintendent to meet our informant who owned a very elegant restaurant occasionally patronised by royalty. I had never seen anything quite like it for expensive decor and was very impressed. We sat down at a small table crammed with free extras such as nuts, sweets, cigarettes, matches, olives, crisps, etc. Had I been paying a bill there I might not have been so enchanted.

Over a delicious lunch we discussed the project in hand. It seemed that the proprietress (one of those small, tough, business-like continental women) objected to the club in question flouting the licensing laws whilst she kept to them like a good girl even though she lost money in the process. But nevertheless she was a member and was willing to get us in that evening. Looking coldly at my simple, grey, Swedish mac' which I thought rather smart and up-to-date, she said, 'What will you be wearing? I am used to taking nicely dressed people you understand?'

Before I had time to answer she continued commandingly, 'I suggest we both wear simple, black dresses. That is the best solution when in doubt.'

I nodded agreement. I did not possess a little black dress and wouldn't have worn it if I had. But the natty, blazer-ed Superintendent was obviously anxious not to upset his good informants and influential friends so I didn't argue – just mentally dug my heels in though my young and vulnerable ego was somewhat bruised.

'I will try to get my husband and his 'fiancée' to come with us. Make a party of it.'

She smiled urbanely at my startled expression.

'Naturally we are all good friends.'

'Naturally,' I gulped.

That evening a tall, pseudo-suave club owner with the requisite continental accent oozed three of us into our seats – the 'good friends' were joining us later. Madame was obviously considered an honoured guest. We dined quite well though certainly not up to

Madame's standards.

I was a little disappointed with the club which was quite elegant but rather dull. A small band in one corner with a longhaired, glitter-besheathed singer and the usual apology for a dance floor.

The charming, tall, dark and quite handsome husband arrived with a surprisingly nice, homely-looking 'other woman' and brightened things up a bit. We knocked back countless bottles of champagne until well after the club's licensed hours. The Sergeant over-acted wildly to convince waiters and the proprietor that he was not a police officer. He needn't have worried, his company and personal appearance did it for him.

The Sarge and I did a couple more observations before the raid night and most of the time I was bored rigid - we had to stay so long. I was even grateful for the diverting company of the resident drunk, a well-to-do middle aged woman.

'I'm waiting for my husband to turn up with his girlfriend,' she told us (what, not even engaged?).

'Of course it's all very civilised,' she said, having a whiskey-ed weep.

'Naturally,' I said.

When the handsome, young, beloved gigolo finally turned up he graced her table for a few minutes before returning to his table and girl-friend.

The next job I did with the Sergeant was at a working men's club. There's glamour for you. To escape such an environment I had fled the North. It was one of the worst examples. Large, bare, hut-like, draughty and uncarpeted. I loathed it. I couldn't imagine why people preferred to drink there instead of in a nice comfy pub, though some seemed to get a thrill out of drinking after hours no matter what the surroundings.

The secretary was a weak and not very bright man who blithely went on serving intoxicating liquor long after his licence allowed. But he was a harmless soul just wanted to be popular. The big disadvantage of clubs work was that if we got to know and like the proprietor and/or customers we felt absolute heels sneaking around telling them lies then later 'shopping' them. Especially when the licensing laws often seemed as trivial to us as they did to them. But 'ours not to reason why' and certainly no one could accuse me of *enjoying* myself at the taxpayers' expense!

On one of the intermittent but seemingly endless nights at this palace of pleasure I noticed several of the men were looking at me speculatively.

'Why am I being gaped at?' I asked the Sergeant.

'Oh, that,' he laughed, 'I was chatting to some of the blokes in the gents. Told them I only go out with you once or twice a week for what I can get. Thought it made a good cover.'

He looked pleased.

Only if you saw the Sergeant could you realise the full insult and (I hope) irony of this statement. I was speechless.

Later I was used for several jobs on my own division, generally in the company of one of two young men. The first was a pleasant, married PC with whom I had little in common and the second was a celebrated bore – well known throughout the division. Only a couple of times did I have the pleasure of being escorted by really personable young officers.

The crashing bore, a tall, red haired Scot, had one topic of conversation: cars. He was obsessed by them. My interest in things mechanical was absolutely nil but rather than sit staring into space for four to six hours (and perhaps jeopardise the job) I would throw in a few 'big ends' and. 'front wheel drives' that had rubbed off on me during conversations with mechanically-minded Bob (who could of course make overhead valves sound fascinating). I had no idea what I was talking about but he was happy and droned on for hours about cam shafts and synchromesh gear boxes.

'Why didn't your colleague see this incident? He was sitting next to you,' asked defence counsel when the case came to court.

'Because he wasn't looking in that direction at the time.'

'Why didn't you draw his attention to it?'

'Well, one must not be too obvious people might notice.'

'But you must have talked to each other. What did you talk about?'

'Cars.'

'What else?'

'Nothing else. Just cars.'

'Do you seriously ask us to believe that you spent all that time together and talked of nothing but cars?'

'Yes.'

Laughter in court – especially from 'C' division fellow-sufferers.

Evidently the truth – tinged with bitterness – shone through. The perplexed counsel abandoned this line of questioning. I didn't know what he was aiming at anyway. Perhaps the usual allegations of collusion. The ways of counsel are devious.

Routine juvenile and missing person enquiries took me into many clubs and restaurants (often in daytime when their glamour was a little frayed around the edges). But once the management of the famous Murrays Cabaret Club invited me to give their cabaret a once over – in the line of duty.

I had stopped a sixteen-year-old girl at 3.30 a.m. one morning in Regent Street. She told me she had just left the club where she was a dancer. She seemed a nice sensible girl but I was nonetheless concerned about the hours and type of show so the following evening a colleague and I went to the club to see the manager. He was charming, helpful and confirmed that the girl worked there.

'But we keep a close eye on the welfare of the girls,' he explained and gave us some examples. 'She only has a small, non-nude part. The woman in charge says her figure is quite unsuitable for nude work. Look, if you're doubtful why not stay and see the show?'

So stay we did. Fortunately, we had come in plain clothes to avoid embarrassment. Though it seemed a bit unorthodox, our purpose was genuine enough. Did the show and her appearing in it constitute a moral danger?

We sat down at a well-placed table in the tiny club and the head waiter brought us a jug of orange juice! The show proved to be glamorous and exotic but really quite innocuous.

Our girl had a small, adequately-clothed role which we decided was O.K.

Our entertainment was enlivened by the attentions of men at the next table who obviously thought us hostesses a bit slow on the uptake.

Women police also went on many club raids. The type of premises varied from the simple drinking club to the full scale night club. I was once involved in a raid on one of the latter, an establishment well known to readers of the Sunday tabloids.

It was dimly lit and glamorous until we put the lights up when it took on a sordid and dingy look. I had been assigned to hostesses, sales girls and dancers and was soon in the thick of acres of exposed bosom. The hostesses told the usual tales of the incredible gullibility of the male patrons who bought them lots of fake drinks, chocolates, stockings, fluffy toys and dolls from the sales girls at fantastic prices. The hostesses later sold these 'presents' back to the club. Sometimes they took men home but only if they fancied them – so they said.

One hostess who looked mid-thirtyish was wearing a suit with an open front fastened with a single button at the waist. Underneath she wore a very low-cut platform bra which shored up her breasts to such an extent that they resembled a couple of overripe pomegranates in imminent danger of bursting. Like those girls in the 'nudie' pictures she seemed to be completely unaware of what was going on from her chin downwards. Perhaps she had merely forgotten to put her blouse on and no one had been decent enough to tell her. Perhaps I should have mentioned it?

When we raided the Ding Dong (technically a 'refreshment house') we took most of the customers into the nick for checking. On raids for breaches of licensing laws customers were not usually involved further than answering questions on what they were drinking, whether they were members, etc. But when club proprietors were being 'done' for harbouring (prostitutes, thieves or absconders) it was of course necessary to prove that some of the customers 'qualified'. So in the Ding Dong raid there were so many to be checked that taking them back to the nick was the only practical thing to do.

At the station we separated the sexes – not as simple as it sounds. One of the girls was a very butch lesbian, so much so that at first we were not quite sure what she was. She wore a complete male outfit. Suit, collar and tie, socks and shoes. And of course a short haircut. When we put all the girls together in a waiting-room there was much flirtatious giggling. 'He' had adopted an exaggerated male attitude and made much play on how lovely it was to be amongst all those beautiful women whilst flirting wildly with both them and us!

Many of the girls seemed flattered by her/his attentions. Her personality was strong and she was far more intelligent and humorous than her companions. She caused so much havoc that eventually we put her in a room by herself.

One pretty, mindless young thing was the lesbian's current girl-friend and was obviously nuts about her though I think that the novelty and sin of it all attracted her as much as the person.

On another raid I was again assigned solely to the women entertainers. They were known as 'shake dancers' – shake being the operative word – dance superfluous. The art consisted of shaking bare or almost bare breasts to music. (I once found it impossible to persuade a mother that her daughter of thirteen who did bare-breasted shake dances in an afternoon drinking club was in moral danger. 'She's only dancing,' mum insisted.)

In this club two women started their wobbling on a tiny stage, then mingled with the clients and shook under their noses. I interviewed the 'dancers' in a bare cubby hole about four feet square behind the stage. They were wearing G-strings but were not bare breasted – they had a tinsel butterfly on each nipple. I winced when I imagined the pulling off and putting on twice or twice nightly.

What I couldn't understand was why the girls were dirty. At close quarters they smelled and had a grimy look. With so little costume maintenance necessary one would think a wash would not have been too much trouble. They swore they enjoyed their work so must have been a trifle exhibitionist. So why not exhibit a clean body?

Whose side was I on anyway?

12
Night Duty 11p.m. - 7a.m.

While I am changing into uniform the Late Turn girls drift in from the streets and chat. The other night duty WPC is already changed and is reading the telephone and telex message books. The Late Turn reserve pops her head round the door.

'Can one of you relieve me in a minute? I'm lumbered with a first time tom.'

'I'll come now,' replies my colleague.

Soon everyone has gone and I pop out to the charge room to lend a hand but she is almost finished. Let's get out on patrol before anything else stops us. Strangely enough when we are on night duty and virtually unsupervised most of us like to go out. Especially at the beginning of the shift. The station officer usually prefers us to stay in so that we are quickly available when he or another station needs a policewoman.

He grumbles a bit as we go out past the front office.

'Keep in touch and don't get yourselves into trouble,' he mutters. We promise to phone in regularly and not to stay out too long.

Down to the Circus and up Shaftesbury Avenue. A prostitute I know quite well does not move like the others but solicits in front of our faces. When I caution her she is cheeky and defiant. We cross the road where a man stops us to ask about all-night buses. Whilst I am answering she solicits again.

That does it! I cross back.

'Right, you're off.'

'What do you mean? You can bloody fuck off!' she shouts, 'I was at court this morning.'

'I mean that I'm arresting you for being a common prostitute soliciting prostitution to the—'

'All right, all right, save it,' she spits, 'I want a cab.'

'We,' I say slowly and firmly, 'are walking.'

This sets off a stream of abuse remarkable only for its staying power – it lasts all the way to the nick.

'You,' she grimaces, 'you're nothing but a fucking little half-pint trying to be a policewoman. You wait until the morning. I'll bring five witnesses to say you're a bleeding liar.'

They are busy downstairs in the male charge room and there are already three toms and a drunk waiting in the female charge room. One of them is an old friend of mine, a soft-voiced, feminine, pretty woman of great charm.

She cringes at Enid's language and raises her elegant eyebrows at me as if to say, 'What are the young prostitutes coming to these days?' She wouldn't dream of behaving like that whatever the circumstances.

Human nature being what it is I treat her differently because she behaves differently but people like her have a much more disturbing effect on my accepted values.

I make notes in my pocket book while I wait for Enid to be charged.

Ah, here's the Sergeant.

'All right, bring on the dancing girls.'

In turn each prisoner sits opposite the charge desk. The officer in the case gives the facts and the station officer decides whether the evidence is sufficient to substantiate the charge. He completes the charge sheet, reads the charge over to the prisoner and cautions her. Any reply is noted by the arresting officer. The matron searches her and all property is carefully listed on the charge sheet. Then the question of bail is gone into – not yet for the drunk of course.

My turn now. I give my evidence. Enid has quite a bit to say in answer to the charge most of it obscene. She is a known prostitute so fingerprints and antecedents are unnecessary.

Nothing else in the nick for us to do so we skip out again smartish. I'm a bit cross, I didn't want to go to court in the morning. It means I won't get to bed until at least 11.30 a.m. and I'm going out tomorrow evening. Still, that's life I guess – police life anyway.

We'll go straight into Soho to the Rio Grande cafe – sleazier than ever at this time of night. But there's no one here whom we don't know. Just as well in a way. It's difficult trying to check on them at this time of night and we've got to have a very good reason to justify keeping them in the station all night. Puts us on the spot if we're not happy about someone but have nothing very strong on them.

On through the quietening streets lined with bins spilling out rubbish, waiting for the morning collections.

Toil up the grubby, dimly-lit stairs to the Ding Dong. Straight into the large, main room. It's packed tonight. Some of the couples dancing hands on bottoms fashion are getting very randy but our presence even though they simulate defiance has a somewhat dampening effect on their ardour. Perhaps it's our cold and steely stare or the way we peer especially carefully at girls whose faces are conveniently hidden in some sweaty shoulder.

I wish they'd turn that wretched juke box down, the throbbing noise is filling my head. Trouble is I know the favourite songs so well I have difficulty in restraining the impulse to sing or nod my head in unison. I certainly follow all the drawn-out notes and pulsating beats mentally.

Often, after leaving, we have a little sing carefully breaking off when drawing parallel with anyone then resuming the suspended song in the same place when a safe distance is reached. It becomes quite an art.

There are so many people in here tonight we have difficulty making sure we don't miss anyone. Sometimes in these places we spot someone we know who is wanted. This happened to me not long ago. I went to the Ding Dong especially to look for a certain girl. I had stopped and arrested her in there as a Borstal escapee two nights previously. When returned to Borstal she had promptly escaped again. So I looked for her. Not missing a face I had squeezed through the crowd. Suddenly, beyond rows of people, I saw her sitting on a window sill. Too late she saw me. I just stood still and beckoned with one finger. She looked around quickly to see whether escape was possible. I shook my head slowly and beckoned again. She shrugged and grinned.

When she reached me we departed the people, heat and music without a word.

'You are daft,' I said later, 'you must have known I'd look for you.'

'Oh, it was a gamble,' she laughed, 'I like it there so I thought I'd chance it. You could have given me a bit more time though.'

Into the back room where the kids neck and suck at straws in Coke bottles which we suspect don't always contain Coke. Lots of hate stares and *sotto voce* cracks here.

We stop a couple of Irish girls and take them outside but their explanations are satisfactory.

Down to Old Compton Street. Hello, there's a small crowd and a lot of noise. Let's investigate. As we get nearer I can see a bobbing helmet and flaying arms appearing now and then in the midst of the people. Without hesitating my mate dashes off to the nearest telephone (the most useful thing anyone can do) and I wade in.

Of course it's a fighting drunk and the crowd has gathered to enjoy the fun and hamper the PC if possible. The baby-faced PC has a good grip on the drunk's arm but the rest of him is flailing about wildly. As I make for his other arm he sees me, lets out a blood-curdling yell and swings it straight at me hitting me on the shoulder and the side of the head. It throws me for a moment but whilst he is concentrating on me the PC is able to get a better grip. I grab for the arm which he's raising above my head and while I'm jumping for it the PC bends him over – got it.

My mate comes back.

'O.K. – van's on the way.'

The three of us back him against the wall and hold him there. If you think it's ridiculous for three people to hold one roaring drunk (without hurting themselves or him) you want to try it some time.

'You want to stick him on for assault?' gasps the panting PC.

'No, don't bother, I'm O.K. and he's just drunk.'

The crowd just stands and stares into our faces even though we tell them to move on and the drunk, now getting his second wind, f—s and blinds at them. The van arrives and he is bundled in unceremoniously.

'Coming?' asks the driver.

'No, we'll walk around a bit more.'

Down Charing Cross Road to Leicester Square the smell of stale onions from one of those hot dog barrows assaults my delicate, night-duty stomach. How people can eat them after smelling that smell and seeing the filthy condition of the barrow and its attendant I really don't know.

Down the toilets. The motherly-figured attendant waddles out to greet us with the familiar cry,

'You should have been down here earlier. One of the girls was drunk and I couldn't get her out.'

'Why didn't you get the male attendant in from next door and ring for us?'

'Well, I didn't like to leave her in here. And anyway if she thought I'd got her arrested she might take it out of me.'

There's a rather noisy group in the wash-room now. We peer in at them.

'They are getting a bit out of hand,' she agrees to our unspoken question.

'Do you want us to turf them out?'

'Well, no,' she looks uneasy. 'Could you just hang around for a bit first – they haven't been in there that long.'

They look well settled in to me but after telling them to cut out the noise we hang around.

After five minutes we go in. There are no bottles visible but the place reeks of drink and sickly perfume.

'Right, you've had long enough to have a bath. Finish off and out you go.'

They start elaborate 'making-up' motions and protest that they have as much right as anyone else to use the wash-room. I agree with them but point out that they've no right to take it over, put the attendant in a difficult position and frighten off potential users. The attendant hovers, looking worried.

We chivvy them out gradually. No sense in treading on their last remnants of pride. They're not really drunk enough to be nicked but enough to be obstreperous (and very obscene) when en masse. They're hovering on the brink and we don't want to provoke them but when we begin to get a little impatient a more sober member of the group sees the danger signal and rounds up the stragglers. They all wander noisily up the stairs as a final protest.

We stay with the attendant for a while after they have gone. Then up and along the front again.

'Evening Officer, evening Officer,' says a high squeaky voice. It's 'Old Feathers' – a vagrant so called because of the feathers he wears all round his hat. He always greets police in this manner.

'Morning Officer, morning Officer,' and so on.

Most 'ordinary' people have gone home now. Only

prostitutes, their friends, layabouts, tom watchers, petty criminals and the like are left – 'the slag' we call them. One common feeling unites these people, they loathe us.

The atmosphere is electric as we pass among them at the narrow point between the front of the London Pavilion and the top of the Underground stairs. They watch us silently, eyes menacingly following our every movement. They want to frighten us, make us feel alone, outcast, threatened. To a certain extent they succeed. But we are outwardly at our most arrogant and unconcerned. I make a quip and we both laugh. This incenses them even more but it's a matter of pride that they should not be seen to get through to us. It's also a matter of safety. Like looking a lion in the eye.

We cross the bottom of Shaftesbury Avenue.

A weedy little Indian approaches. 'I am wanting my money back,' he whines, 'I paid a prostitute and didn't get my satisfaction. I did not have enough time.'

'Hard luck,' I say curtly.

'You must do something or I will report you.'

'Please yourself.'

I turn away. This is a regular complaint to police and it annoys me. It is also the only circumstance where I fail to take any action. I am supposed to refer him to his civil remedy, i.e. that he has the right to sue her in a civil court. And I should see that names and addresses are exchanged, then make out a report on the incident.

I've risked my job a couple of times by telling these men to get lost. I go a long way in subjecting my own feelings and standards when 'doing my duty' but this is where I draw the line. I refuse to act as mediator in these sordid little contracts and I think it's very undignified and insulting to the police and the law to expect us to do this. Of course I am technically wrong in not taking any action. I should do everything I am paid to do.

He is still mumbling but I ignore him. My colleague is talking to a French couple who can't get a cab though there are quite a few about, mostly empty, but without their 'For Hire' signs illuminated. *We* know why this is. They are waiting to pick up prostitutes and their clients to take them to a nearby quiet street or square. Intercourse will take place in the back of the cab and the cabbie will get a very large 'tip' without expending much energy or petrol. Very profitable. Of course this is illegal and they can be prosecuted but they make sure they are not caught.

We spot a 'For Hire' cab which has paused at the kerb nearby and with our enquirers walk quickly to it. We stand by whilst they give their destination to the driver who, with us there, daren't refuse the fare. Off they go, puzzled but grateful.

We wander over to. Swan and Edgar's and phone the nick. The van is standing here on its nightly 10 p.m. to 2 a.m. watch, a more central position for a dash to wherever needed.

We are wanted. A woman prisoner awaits collection from Tottenham Court Road, the other station on our sub-division. Their matron is off sick. We stroll back to the nick.

In Regent Street we stop for a word with a huge man with long, black, curly hair, a friendly soul who is acting as night watchman to a hole in the road. We know him well, he often supplements his income with pavement art in Trafalgar Square.

We get quite attached to our characters. In addition to those already mentioned there is 'Old Vera' – a vagrant type who is the usual bundle of clothes on the outside but is reputed to have very clean underwear which she washes in the toilets.

Then there is the man who strides unseeing down the street, his long, grey hair streaming out behind him. I was told that he walks from Shepherds Bush almost every evening and visits all the cinemas in the West End looking for his son who was killed when a bomb fell on a cinema queue during the war.

I must mention our Chinaman who dresses in brocade tunic and trousers and a coolie hat. His outfit is completed by a number eight battery which is suspended over his forehead! 'Whenever you see him,' say the more knowing PCs, 'you can be sure it's going to rain.'

Of course we have our less pleasant characters. From time to time women complain about one scruffy old vagrant who always carries a bottle on a piece of string. It contains urine. Every now and then he chases a lady brandishing this and muttering to himself. He believes that his bottle is his dog. A bored, night-duty PC once found the old man asleep in a doorway so crept up and took the bottle. Then he woke the old man up and told him his dog had been stolen. Much blaspheming ensued while the PC laughed his head off. He eventually returned the old man's 'pet' before going on his way.

Amongst the regular street entertainers is a very good traditional jazz band. They are favourites with police because they play good music and cause little obstruction by always keeping on the move. They walk slowly along the edge of the kerb, usually in Oxford Street, blowing and strumming away – and raking in the shekels.

Around Leicester Square at week-ends the 'Chain Gang' are usually to be found. One of them strips to the waist, is manacled and shackled, placed in a sack which is then wrapped in chains – two crossed swords completing the fastening. The rest of the show – which is drawn out as long as possible whilst money is collected – is the prisoner's 'dramatic escape'.

There are also the occasionals such as 'Spoons' who, as his name suggests, plays the spoons and quite well too, and a man who stands on his head on a glass tumbler in the middle of the street amidst whirling traffic.

Our most regular woman drunk known to everyone – is a raddled old prostitute said to have been a real beauty in her day. She is mostly a rip-roaring, obscene-mouthed, copper-hating drunk. But sometimes she gets maudlin and always sends a Christmas card to 'Les girls at West End Central'. She is not alone in this. At Christmas the notice board in our canteen is always decorated with cards from street traders, entertainers, street photographers and drunks.

'You'll have to walk up there, all the cars and vans are out,' says the station officer.

But one of the area wireless cars is outside the station as we leave.

'Going to give us a lift to Tottenham Court Road?'

'Sure, if you can wait a couple of minutes. Our observer's just gone in to clear the last call.'

We sit in the back and are soon joined by the plain clothes observer. Three men operate these cars the driver, the radio operator and the PC in plain clothes who sits in the back and, as his title suggests, 'observes'. The only trouble with getting a lift from them is that one can be dumped unceremoniously at any point should an urgent call come through. But this time we get there without a hitch. They are quite pleased to see the female of the species and are very chatty.

We take the sleepy prisoner back in their prison van.

3.30 a.m. and I'm hungry. Time to have some grub. A bit late tonight though. Some nights we are lucky to grab any. One never knows whether the night will be absolutely uneventful or provide enough work for six WPCs.

While we eat we are visited by one or two of the blokes.

Drivers, CID and the occasional PC. They prefer our tea to the canteen variety and also like a bit of feminine company, especially the unmarried section-house boys who live, eat, sleep and work among hordes of men. They are interested in us as normal young men are interested in young women. But to our surprise we sometimes find ourselves acting as substitute mums to some of them and are the recipients of some quite surprising confidences in the early hours when resistance is low and the atmosphere intimate. After all, some of them are only nineteen and amongst themselves men must keep up this tough male image.

The drivers just come up for a gossip. They get lonely in their underground office.

Bob comes in for his grub. I tell him I'm lumbered for court in the morning.

'So am I,' he grins.

'Which one?'

'Bow Street.'

'Oh good, that'll cheer me up.'

5.30 a.m. We go for a walk. Dawn is just breaking. How I love this time of the morning. The air is sparkling and fresh, the streets clean from the attentions of the Westminster City Council and bare of the daytime hordes. A quiet, private world. We step it out with gusto. The occasional early morning person is about: a cleaner, milkman, filler of window boxes, etc. The water cart is still doing its ablutive round. Everyone speaks to everyone at this hour. Not to do so seems unnatural.

Mayfair is at its best now so we head in that direction. A little orgy of window gazing, then on towards Grosvenor Square where the early morning sun is glancing off the dark houses and lighting their meticulously painted doors and windows – this is twee-land.

We pay a courtesy call on the bored guardian of the American Embassy. With his truncheon he is the first line of defence. The second line (inside) is two American marines armed with revolvers. Even if the PC was armed (as on an occasional 'trouble-spot' embassy) he would be instructed to keep his revolver well out of sight so as not to disturb the delicate public image and not to shoot until shot at!

He is delighted to have visitors and stuffs his science fiction paperback into his pocket. It was half way there when he heard our approach. In common with sentries the world over his palm is browned by the practice of concealed smoking. He tells us how many times that Belisha beacon flashes in a year and how many panes of glass there are in the buildings on his side of the square. We are duly impressed.

His job is worst in winter. They get very cold standing around all the time. Once, for a short while, this was alleviated by sympathetic Americans who put an electric fire outside trailing the flex through the letter-box! Of course this was soon discovered by our hierarchy and discontinued.

Having done our social duty we visit President Roosevelt resplendent in white stone as he presides over the flowers and impeccable lawns of the Square gardens. Then on past one of London's top hotels. On late turn recently we had a cuppa there in high style. I was with Shirl who, like all self-respecting Australians, knows everyone including the banqueting manager of this top hotel, Claridges. We stopped to chat with him and were invited in for a quick cup of tea. We received many such invitations but rarely accepted.

He led us through to an empty, secluded dining-room and sat us at a table beautifully laid out with silver service. Our eyes popped as a waitress appeared with huge silver dishes of strawberries, cream and ice-cream. Another waitress dashed round pouring out tea, laying napkins over our uniforms and bringing platters of those delicious petit fours that the big hotels make so well. We were soon giggling at the sheer incongruity and naughtiness of it all. The strawberries and cream were delicious and we put away as many of the petit fours as we could manage.

'Take the rest with you,' said the manager supplying a paper napkin. We staggered back to the nick that night for a tea break trying not to look too replete and when Sarge was out of the room we fed the rest of the green-eyed relief on the sweetmeats.

Down through the backstreets to 'Piccadilly Dip' (where the street slopes into a hollow alongside Green Park). Lately, soliciting by male prostitutes in the dip has been getting almost as bad as the female variety elsewhere but at this time it's blessedly empty. Along to the Circus where we 'do' the toilets which are now open. The Circus denuded of snarling traffic and still wet from the water carts is the best sight of all. Back to the nick. The only cloud on my horizon is that tom.

One of the best things about night duty is snuggling down into bed when everyone else is reluctantly getting up. Now I am in the usual cleft stick. Should I go back to the Section House? I could be there by seven-thirty. But I have to be back at the nick two hours later to change into uniform and book on before walking over to Bow Street for Court.

If I go back to the Section House I shall be tempted to lie down 'for a minute'. The last time I did that I woke at nine-thirty and arrived in Court just as my prisoner was leaving the dock! Fortunately she had pleaded guilty and no one had missed me, except for the Court Inspector that is, who was furious and refused to sign my court card.

I did just the same when due at Juvenile Court one day. I had exhorted the parents to be there early because I was on nights and might be able to get the case brought forward. They were there on the dot of ten-thirty – I arrived an hour later. They were amused and sympathetic but my Inspector wasn't.

I suppose I could have a bath and freshen up at the Section House. If I remain at the station I'll have to spend two and a half hours in the women police office.

I settle for the bath.

Early turn reserve arrives at 6.45 a.m. and changes quickly so we get away early.

'Have a good sleep,' she says cheerily.

I look sour.

13
Courting

I wend my way past the fruit and flower boxes in Covent Garden en route to Bow Street Magistrates Court. I run the gauntlet of chirpy wisecracks and comment from the inimitable market men.

'Mornin' darlin', who've you been pinchin'?'

'Come on, 'urry up, the beak's just sat down.'

"Ave an orange, gu^y? Two oranges? A box of oranges?'

'You can tell she's an 'ard woman, can't you Fred?'

'Protect me, darlin'.'

One clasps his chest and does a mock faint at the sight of me. I can't help laughing.

I feel I belong here, the atmosphere of warmth and good-humoured awareness envelops me. They take the mickey more than anyone else but have the perception and lightness of touch that prevents it ever being objectionable – affectionate rather. The traffic jams are hideous but they sort themselves out.

Bow Street Court and the adjoining nick stand in the middle of this picturesque chaos. The front of the station boasts a *white* lamp – a sort of goldfish bowl and wrought iron affair – which was erected after Queen Victoria visited the Opera opposite and decreed that the traditional blue lamp was unbecoming!

Into the court building, across the hall, down a long corridor and into the gaoler's office. Doors are open as the prisoners are still in the cells. I check which court I'm in and my whereabouts on the list. I leave my court card with the Inspector in Court One. This shows him that I'm here, he signs the card to that effect and signs again when I leave so that I get credited with the overtime which I can take off later.

I peek into the waiting-room – O.K., mine's there, she's already surrendered to her bail. My God, doesn't she look ghastly first thing in the morning all whey-faced. She glares at me. I try to remain expressionless.

Just a matter of hanging around now until the Court starts.

I have done matron duty occasionally at Marlborough Street Magistrates Court, the other court we attend and which is actually situated on our own ground, beside the Palladium. Cell-land is a dark world of locked doors, dim lights, white-tiled cells and corridors (like vast toilets), cream paintwork and toilet flushes which are huge metal sliders set in the walls (no chains inside for obvious reasons).

The gaoler brings the 'overnights' from the cells and hands each one over to the officer in the case who is now responsible for his safe custody. I'd better collect dear Enid and get into the queue outside the courtroom. She's petulant but resigned. I don't see any of her five witnesses.

Mr Blundell is on the bench; he combines kindness with firmness in the best possible way and is always courteous, especially to women police.

We are fortunate to have stipendiary magistrates at both our courts. This means in effect that one professional sits on each bench instead of three amateurs. A collective noun coined by one sarcastic PC to describe the latter is 'A travesty of Justices!'

Only occasionally does a bench of JPs sit here and they are better than most probably because of the example of the 'proper' magistrates and the fact that the Central London venue means more Press attention. As far as we're concerned the big difference is that the stipendiary is quicker, less gullible (they've often dealt personally when they were counsel with the types who come before them) and on the whole are less liable to be swayed by their personal prejudices. This can be of equal benefit to the accused.

A very shame-faced, bleary-eyed Irishman approaches me. 'Is it true what the fella here says? I belted you one last night?'

'Yes, it certainly is! You're lucky I didn't stick you on for assault – magistrates don't like people who hit women police,' I reply with mock sternness. He looks mortified.

'Jeez, I'm sorry, I don't remember a thing about it. Did I hurt you?'

I take pity on his embarrassment.

'No, of course not, it was watered down by the Irish whiskey.'

He grins deferentially at my bit of Irish logic and retires, shaking his head.

Ah, here's Bob a bit pushed. He collects his drunk and joins the queue a bit behind me. Enid and I are number six on the list, Bob is number fourteen – the first of the drunks. The lists are always in the same order quick simple charges first. Prostitutes, drunks, obstructions (mostly street traders), insulting words and/or behaviour (the 'breathing act' which covers all sorts of conduct liable 'to provoke a breach of the peace'), three-card tricksters and then the crime, this last usually starting with the International Shoplifting Brigade.

The list then works its way through the 'big stuff' – more serious larcenies, false pretences, break-ins, woundings, and so on. It was surprising the number of people who failed to realise that *all* offenders came to Magistrates Courts first and then a proportion were 'sent up the road' (to Sessions or the Old Bailey) either for sentence or having been committed for trial.

Right, we're off. I'm nervous, I'm always nervous. If Enid pleads 'not guilty' (which seems likely) I'll have to stand up in the witness box and give full evidence. I hate that, all eyes on me. Never would have made an actress. Nonetheless, a straightforward 'not guilty' is not like facing counsel (though she could bring one if she wanted to). After hearing the truth mutilated so expertly one can begin to wonder if one was at the incident at all. The dreaded cross-examination when one knows counsel's sole aim (especially if there is no defence to speak of) is to discredit utterly: to make one look stupid, a liar or at least completely unreliable. And don't think this can't happen to an intelligent and responsible person who is telling the truth. It can. Fortunately, magistrates have seen this sort of attack so many times that it often nullifies itself.

In and out of Court go prostitute, officer, prostitute, officer – it's like a conveyor belt. My turn now, into a crowded court. Enid goes into the nearby dock while I walk quickly across the back on my way round to the witness box. The charge is read. To my relief I hear a cross 'Guilty'.

'Anything to say?'

'No.'

'Pay forty shillings, please.'

She's leaving the dock as I reach the back of the witness box. I collect the charge sheet from the clerk and follow Enid out to the gaoler who collects the money. Formalities over I go back into Court.

Think I'll wait for Bob. All seats are taken so I stand.

I love to watch court proceedings, the interest never wanes. A prostitute pleads 'not guilty' so the flow is stemmed for a while. I'm feeling a bit tired now and I've got night duty 'doesn't know what it wants' stomach and a 'bottom of a birdcage' mouth.

Bob's drunk comes in, pleads 'guilty' and is fined five shillings. Bob is much more confident in the box than I am but then he's more experienced and a bit of an exhibitionist at heart!

'Coming for a cup, luv?'

'Well, we should get away to bed. Oh, all right.'

Bow Street nick's canteen is full of friends and we chat, feeling wide-awake now in that nervous, unreal way. Half-an-hour later we leave. Should get to bed by half past twelve.

14
Training

My three months' initial training took place at Peel House, an ancient building in Victoria. The Metropolitan Police had a modern training school at Hendon but this was for men only.

Most WPCs were accommodated at a special training school section house near Baker Street but when I arrived it was full so the large contingent of WPCs (eight) in my class was put into Tooting Section House. It was more difficult to study in the noisy, unsympathetic environment but far more comfortable. We were taken to and fro each day by coach.

The men (poor things) lived in the cubicles at Peel House – dubbed 'stationary cattle trucks' by one of the tutors.

The day at training school always commenced with a parade in the yard, each class in a separate line with its own class captain and right marker to whom we all 'squared up'. The superior senior classes were at the front and the self-consciously new to the rear.

The men were issued with their off-the-peg uniforms straight away but our tailor-mades didn't arrive until we were near the end of our three months, so we took longer to assume our new identities. But our collars, ties, hats, shoes and stockings and macs were all standard issue so we wore these for parade and in the classrooms a civilian skirt with our collar and tie. The men in our class were for ever re-tying our ties and polishing the peaks of our caps with sergeant-major-like barks – 'looks as though you've been having your dinner off it!'

The quality of all our uniform was vastly superior to that of the men and there seemed to be so much of it. To stave off inclement weather we were issued with one tailor-made top coat, which was smart on taller girls but its square shoulders made me look like a cube; one gaberdine mac and one riding mac to cope with heavier rain and cold winds. Plus wellingtons, hideous galoshes and last but not least, our 'foreign legions'. The latter fitted over our caps and floated free at the back just like those worn by the desert warriors except that ours were meant to keep us dry. They were the only means (and a not very effective one) of protecting our hair from the rain but if we were not careful they channelled it neatly down our necks. We soon decided that nothing looked worse than straggly hair with uniform – except a 'foreign legion'.

We felt such fools wearing them. PCs choked with laughter at the sight and even the public sometimes made 'witty' remarks. So, being vain women, we wore them only in direst emergencies.

Our course was three months of hard mental graft with oceans of stuff to be learnt parrot fashion and hours of homework every evening. The rather dull lessons were livened up by racy 'beat' anecdotes designed to wake us up and to shock the WPCs ('in preparation for the wicked world outside' was the excuse and some of the innocents needed it).

Intermingled throughout the course were mock incidents, lectures and practice in first-aid, Civil Defence (such a bore), self-defence and drill. (The men hated having eight girls in the middle to spoil their clever, a la National Service marching – most classes had only two or three such encumbrances). There were visits from accident ambulances and police cars, mock courts (an agony of embarrassment for me), lectures from murder squad and forensic scientists and tests, tests, tests. A photographic memory was often of more use than intelligence but, like the late distinguished broadcaster Kenneth Allsop, I have 'instant forget'.

One instructor remarked comfortingly, 'Don't worry, the women always make a fuss but they always pass. They are handpicked not just any old rubbish like the men!'

The reason that they could handpick us was that they needed such a small number and there were few other interesting jobs for women so they could pick and choose which applicants they wanted. We women were a mixed lot but in the main were ex-secretaries, bank-clerks, teachers and nurses. There were three of us State Registered Nurses (SRNs) in Peel House whilst I was there – one of whom caused a furore by failing her first-aid exam! Like the men, we came from all parts of the British Isles – the Met. being the most mixed force in the country in this respect.

But our instruction and exams did not cease when we arrived on division. For the first two years we were probationers, attended weekly lectures and sat two big exams, one at nine months' and the other at fifteen months' service. Our instructors and immediate seniors submitted monthly progress reports on us and, during the probationary period, we could be chucked out for failure in the exams or simply for being 'unlikely to become an efficient constable'.

In addition to coping with normal police duties, women police were considered to be specialists in dealing with women and children, so we had two additional courses to this end: a junior (two week) course shortly after arrival on division and a senior (three week) course at the end of our second year. On these we found it interesting to meet girls from other divisions and compare notes. Unlike us who worked in the West End some of the women regularly dealt with quite horrifying child neglect cases, others were always being dragged into family disputes or becoming involved in sordid sex cases. To me one surprising fact which emerged from these chats was the very high incidence of incest both in working class and 'respectable' suburban areas. Usually between father and daughter and sometimes with mother's knowledge!

These courses were the usual mixture of interest and sheer boredom. But the women police hierarchy did a good job in breaking up the dull stuff with lectures by all sorts of interesting people and taking us on educational visits which widened our knowledge about the general public so that we became far more informed about them than our average male counterparts.

We had lectures from psychiatrists, top CID men, experts on drugs, probation officers, the WVS, the Salvation Army, Immigrant Liaison Workers, Divorce Court Experts, the NSPCC, Children's Officers, Youth Employment Workers, Doctors (VD and the Prostitute), and youth workers. We were also given lectures on the work of women police in the provinces and in other countries and were shown a film on unaided childbirth.

Visits were arranged to the 'Black Museums' at Hendon. and Scotland Yard, Approved Schools, Borstals and Holloway Prison. I had already been to Holloway and several other prisons whilst on prison van duty but only to collect and discharge prisoners. Now we did a grand tour with polite but overworked prison officers as our guides. We were strictly warned to speak to no one even if we recognised them. But they recognised us. Although we were in plain clothes as soon as we entered Holloway Prison one of a small group of prisoners said, 'Here's some of the girls from West End Central.'

Most unnerving.

We 'did' the prison's marmalade factory, the mail-bag-making and wireless-dismantling departments. I found the 'spider's web' corridors and steel stairways in the main building most intimidating. Naturally I found the hospital and its arrangements very interesting. I mused on the intricacies of unlocking and re-locking a door whilst carrying a used bedpan.

15
Escort Duty

'Ever been to Wales?'

'No.'

'Right, we'll soon rectify that. Your train leaves in an hour and a half. You're taking a juvenile to a remand home in Barry, Glamorganshire. Oh, take a toothbrush you're staying the night.'

This was my greeting when I reported for late turn one sunny, summer afternoon. Of course I had to be wearing my white twinset for the second time. It would be all right, I had thought, for 'dirtying out' in the hour it took to and from work. I would look really charming by this time tomorrow after two train journeys.

Lockers were searched and a set of toiletries scraped together, the canteen supplied toothbrushes and we were all set for sophisticated travel. Usually we had a little more notice than this. Sometimes even a whole day!

The purpose of most long-distance escort duties was to facilitate the transfer of offenders from the area in which they had been apprehended to that in which they committed the offence or return them to custody. The escort was usually supplied by the force which 'wanted' the prisoner. Occasionally, when our remand homes were full, we escorted juveniles to one outside the Metropolitan Police District – as in this Barry trip.

One of my more unusual escort sorties was to a northern industrial city to execute a Care or Protection warrant. Some weeks previously one of our WPCs had stopped Mary (the girl named in the warrant) because of her youth, the lateness of the hour and the undesirable company she was keeping. Care or Protection proceedings were not justified at that stage, she was just a 'possible' for the future. Mary complained bitterly at our action and was supported by her father who thought we were making a fuss about nothing. The girl even got a solicitor to send a letter accusing the WPC of slapping her and threatening litigation if we continued to molest her!

Not long after this the father called at the station. We must help him. He didn't know what to do about his daughter. He had come to us because we knew her! We took our tongues out of our cheeks and extracted the full story.

Mary had gone off with three men in a stolen car and had taken her father's gun with her. They had driven all over the country and ended up in the northern city where the men had been arrested on a charge of conspiracy to rob a local business of a reputed fifty thousand pounds. The girl had turned Queen's evidence and was not being charged. She was now residing with a prostitute. Father wanted her back. 'Told you so' seemed inadequate.

'We could take the fairly unusual step of obtaining a Care or Protection warrant.'

'Yes, yes. Anything.'

When we arrived the local CID Sergeant escorted a colleague and myself to the prostitute's 'drum' in what he called a 'right rough area'. All the areas looked rough to me. While we executed the warrant the blow was softened by the Detective Sergeant who was understandably trying to keep his star witness 'sweet'. She was soon wallowing in all the attention and behaved well on the return journey, reading magazines (provided by the Sergeant) and regaling us with tales of fights (physical) she had had with a prostitute over her ponce. It seemed the ponce preferred Mary to his prostitute – a fact of which Mary was very proud.

There are two things to watch out for on escort duty attempts to escape or commit suicide. The latter is less likely but it does happen. We travelled as ordinary passengers but the railway police would do their best to get us a private compartment. We did not use handcuffs (they were rarely issued in the Met. Police). Losing a prisoner was considered a heinous police crime thus escapes from police custody were rare. Yet when they do happen will 'keep you writing' for ever. We could not afford to let our charges out of our sight for a second. Not even to go to the lavatory. One of our WPCs missed a connection because she failed to put her foot in the toilet door. The girl promptly locked it and refused to come out. By the time the railway officials had extracted her the connecting train had left. Even so, the WPC was lucky. That particular girl had no suicidal tendencies!

Fortunately, Mary and I got on fairly well for we were to spend more train hours together. Six months after we brought her from the north my superiors decided I needed to visit Barry again – this time as Mary's escort.

When she was dealt with for Care or Protection the juvenile court placed her under a Supervision Order and she returned home. Mary renewed her acquaintance with the police when she began soliciting prostitution in Hyde Park. She was taken before the juvenile court for breach of the Supervision Order and the magistrates remanded her in custody while they considered their next move. Hence the trip to the remand home.

She greeted me like a long lost friend.

'How's your boy-friend? Still got the motor bike?' The juveniles often showed an avid interest in our personal life and remembered any little snippet of information we let drop. En route to Barry Mary expounded her philosophies.

'Prostitution's not as bad as they make out. I get lots of laughs you know.'

She proceeded to illustrate her point. One of her clients (she swore this was true) required her to sit with him in the front of his car. She wore a fur coat (provided by him) over her naked body and a swimming cap on her head. They then took each other's temperatures and if hers rose a little higher (highly unlikely I would have thought) he was satisfied. That's all. She received five pounds.

Another client who amused her was a young man who always became full of remorse *after* intercourse in the back of his van and wanted to 'take her away from all this' as she was 'a nice girl really'. She thought he was daft.

Mary had been living with a coloured man and was enthusiastic about his sexual prowess.

'It's true what they say once you've been with one you don't want white men anymore.'

She poured forth all this edifying information without any prompting. But my very new, very young, and now very wide-eyed companion began encouraging her which I felt was lowering to our dignity and certainly bad for the girl.

'That's enough,' I said as I gave the WPC an icy look and feigned disinterest in any further revelations.

I took Mary for some refreshments. Her fairly ordinary face was devoid of make-up, her mousy hair straight and her jumper and skirt very plain. She had that slightly seedy look of someone in custody. Nevertheless every male eye was upon her well-developed figure. She oozed sex. I became quite non-existent. She stuck out her bust and preened. I wondered how many girls were as happy in and suited to their chosen employment as Mary was to prostitution.

Barry was a holiday resort (to me bleak and joyless in a way that only certain British resorts can be) and a port. In complete contrast the remand home was in the attractive countryside a short way from the town. We approached through wide-open gates and knocked on the door. No answer. All was silence in this sylvan retreat. The place seemed deserted.

'Just the spot for little me,' grinned Mary, reading my thoughts.

At last a pleasant, smiling woman appeared and apologised for keeping us waiting. 'It's tea-time,' she explained.

That was the last I saw of Mary although I heard that on her return to Court she 'got approved school'.

Short distance escort duties were part of our everyday life. We took women prisoners to Court when they could not be picked up by the prison van, women in custody when the CID wished to search their homes in their presence or take them to the venue of an offence, escapees who were being returned to mental homes, shoplifters from store to station, juveniles from station to remand homes pending their initial appearance at Court, and countless other women and children for divers reasons.

We also had an occasional day on the juvenile van which transported children to Court from remand home and return, or on the prison van which carried out a similar function for adults. Neither of these duties was very popular as each required our presence at Lambeth Garage (an awkward place to get to) at seven in the morning.

There was also the clothing problem.

For juvenile van we had to wear plain clothes. Simple enough but there were a few rules. Firstly, those in charge had a 'thing' about hats. When receiving our post training school interview with Miss Bather (then Superintendent of Women Police) we were required to wear plain clothes —and a hat. Not to have worn one would have shown a complete lack of respect. Many of us did not possess a hat (especially as bouffant hair styles were current fashion) and were therefore obliged to buy one for the occasion. Everyone then possessed a 'Miss Bather hat'. This rule applied to all plain clothes escort duty. To look dignified and to differentiate between ourselves and the prisoner or juvenile we must wear a hat.

A 'Miss Bather hat' was quite dressy as one naturally wears one's best for 'Boss meeting'. Unfortunately, flat shoes were another (but more sensible) escort essential. We would be at a disadvantage in high heels if a fracas broke out or if (God forbid) we had to pursue a prisoner.

The clothing in between needed to be casual, able to adapt to whatever weather made its appearance between dawn and dusk, not look like a rag after a day in the van, be child-proof, give freedom of movement (for comfort and prisoner-chasing) and be dignified. Add the dressy hat and flat shoes and you have a fashion editor's nightmare. Many girls bought a more casual hat but it still looked pretty silly.

No one had the courage openly to flout the rule even though it could really be termed an unlawful order as we were not reimbursed. But many of us indulged in quiet sabotage. We carried the hat and if we thought it likely that we would meet a superior officer (woman-type) we popped it on. This became quite a game. Most days we wouldn't see any rank but sometimes we were caught off guard and, if unlucky, reported.

'I hear you were caught without a hat on juvenile bus the other day,' our Inspector would say in a shocked voice.

We travelled quite long distances in the square, green, juvenile van (dubbed 'the chocolate box' by the kids), often into the countryside around London. We visited remand homes, courts and police stations of all sizes and types. I felt tempted to produce a Bad Food Guide to Metropolitan Police Canteens' (actually they varied from the very good to the utterly appalling).

The juveniles were fairly easy to handle en masse though the girls would often yell and make signs at any vaguely attractive man or boy as we passed. Hard, risqué conversation was considered very smart. I never restrained them unless they became very noisy, unruly or obscene.

One day we picked up a quiet, eight-year-old boy (the older boys were handled separately) and the girls started their sexy talk. Before I had time to speak they were admonished by one of their worst offenders.

'You mustn't speak like that in front of the child!'

They stopped immediately and mothered the startled boy for the rest of the journey.

Prison van escort duties by women police were commenced half-way through my service as the result of a newspaper report giving prominence to a complaint by a woman prisoner that she had heard swearing from the male prisoners whilst being conveyed in the van (this later led to women prisoners being conveyed separately in a 'chocolate box'). We were never quite sure what difference our presence was supposed to make. Nothing could stop the men swearing if they felt like it — we couldn't even tell which cell it was coming from. So we all thought it pretty farcical and one day whilst standing by the driver's cab I said as much to the van Sergeant.

'Makes me laugh, putting us on these vans to try to prevent these innocent ladies hearing swear words. Most of them could teach the men a few!'

A raucous scream came from inside the van.

'We can hear you! Bleeding superior cow who the fucking hell do you think you are?'

I loathed prison van duty. The only provision for a second escort was a small, uncomfortable tip-up seat at the very back. The line of vision was straight up the dreary central corridor between the tiny cells. A small window behind allowed a draught to blow directly on to the back of one's neck and the ride (outside the wheelbase) was bumpy! The prisoners were more confined but they did not have to spend the whole day there. A few kindly van Sergeants allowed us to sit on an upturned box by the driver or in the front cell (if unoccupied obviously), our legs keeping the door ajar. Both places were *verboten* (accident risk) and uncomfortable but at least we could see outside a little.

The huge vans fanned out to different prisons, loaded up their cargo of miscreants then converged on certain selected police stations which possessed large, lockable yards. Here, there was much swapping around until each van had its quota for the courts in a particular area. It was a fascinating, well-planned jigsaw. We also collected any 'overnight' prisoners from police stations.

For ordinary duties we changed into uniform on arrival at the station but on prison van escort it was necessary to travel to work in uniform. This was a great disadvantage as we were liable to get involved in all sorts of incidents and be asked questions in areas where we might not even know the whereabouts of the nearest police station! I've been stopped in Charing Cross Underground Station when en route for home and a queue has formed in front of me waiting to ask 'which platform' questions. We always felt obliged to answer if possible – the absence of the duty armband meant nothing to the public.

When passing through in unknown territory I usually affected a brisk, determined, 'on an urgent call' walk. In Pimlico one day the inevitable workman spotted me from his hole in the road.

'Wouldn't mind being arrested by you,' he shouted breezily. 'A fair cop!'

I grinned at him without breaking my step then averted my head for a quick, relieving 'Stupid idiot' – straight into the astonished face of a woman who had just opened her ground floor window! I must have blushed beetroot as I did a rapid 'eyes front' and quickened my pace to a near-gallop.

The escorting of aliens to embarkation points sometimes came our way. I accompanied one such to London Airport. I did not know the reasons for deportation but understood it to be a routine job. We were usually very liberal on this score compared with many other countries. But, as the result of a somewhat dramatic story about her arrest in the provinces appearing in the *Daily Express*:

'YOU ARE TO BE DEPORTED –
BE READY IN ONE HOUR.'
SOBBING AND PROTESTING MRS —
PLEADED FOR MORE TIME

And a quote from the daughter:

'IT IS A TERRIBLE SHOCK.
WE THOUGHT THIS
WAS A FREE COUNTRY.'

We were warned that we might be subjected to a great deal of Press attention.

I had to be at the nick at six in the morning to give us plenty of time to get through formalities before she was placed on the nine o'clock flight for Vienna. My disgust at being up at such an uncivilised hour was obviously shared by the rather weary-looking girl reporter who rushed forward as we left the station. I was prepared to hold her at bay but the suave PC from Aliens Office said, 'It's all right, let her speak to the woman.'

The reporter looked suspicious but fired questions as I ushered the alien into the car and continued the barrage through the open window. The alien a forty-seven year old Jugoslav-born stateless person looked at her blankly. She didn't understand a word of English.

'I might have known there was a catch,' said the reporter cynically and she ran to her car as we started to drive away. She followed us all the way to the airport and caught us as we entered the building. My shrewd colleague chatted to her quite charmingly.

'We're going for a cup of tea. You can join us if you like provided that you don't attract the attention of any of your colleagues who may be lying in wait.'

Delighted, she assured us she wouldn't. We passed through the foyer unmolested and she was rather chuffed when she recognised a group of lounging newspapermen none of whom spotted us.

'They wouldn't be expecting three women and one man,' whispered Frank craftily.

We had a life-saving cup of tea while the girl bemoaned the fact that though so near she could not communicate with the alien. Frank 'wished he could help' but 'could not communicate either'. He charmingly told her 'all he knew' which conveniently turned out to be not much.

Marjorie Morningstar was not fooled but accepted defeat gracefully. This good-looking officer was so friendly and courteous and at least she'd got nearer than the others.

Maria, the alien, who appeared to be quite happy throughout all this, suddenly dashed out on to a terrace closely followed by Frank. She came back after a few minutes all smiles.

'What's pleased her?' asked the reporter.

'Oh, she's never seen planes so close before, she was quite interested.'

'Really? How do you know? You no speaka the same language?'

'Oh, the odd word and sign language,' he grinned. 'Well, we'd better make a move.'

We were allowed to use a VIP lounge and soon the airport's own press man came to see us. Frank consented to his talking with her providing he didn't upset her. A hurried search was made for an interpreter and one duly arrived whilst Frank was away attending to some official details. They started to question her and she seemed quite happy but when they persisted in trying to get her reaction to leaving her son and daughters she started to cry. An agitated young man in uniform appeared from nowhere and demanded to know what was going on. I told him.

'But we can't have her crying in *here!*' he said aghast. 'You must stop her or you'll have to leave.'

Frank re-appeared at the crucial moment, stopped the questioning, got the interpreter to quieten her down and by the time the departure was announced she was 'quite looking forward to the flight'.

On the way to the plane the camera bulbs popped as we walked down the glass-walled corridors and again at the foot of the plane's steps. Maria and I appeared in a later edition of the *Evening Standard* together with a fairly-controlled factual piece on the incident.

The next day the *Manchester Guardian* devoted some of its front page to comments by the chairman of the Liberal Party Civil Liberties Committee with the headings,

'EARLY MORNING KNOCK'
'GESTAPO METHODS' IN DEPORTATION'

It quoted the chairman describing the deportation as

'GESTAPO AND OGPU METHODS IN GREAT BRITAIN'

and went on :

'HERE ARE ALL THE TRAPPINGS
OF THE POLICE STATE – THE EARLY
MORNING KNOCK'–

(now I agree – *anything* to do with early morning is evil) –

'A HALF HOUR TO DRESS AND PACK'

The *Daily Express* gave her an hour–

'THE CAR RIDE TO A SECRET DESTINATION'

(So secret that the daughter was taken to visit her at OGPU headquarters – our nick – an hour and a half later).

'THE EJECTION OF A DAUGHTER
FROM THE CAR BEFORE IT REACHED
ITS DESTINATION'

Not, as you might be forgiven for thinking, flung bloodied on to the road but, to quote daughter in the *Daily Express* again:

'I was allowed to travel with my mother on one condition –
that I would leave the car before it reached its destination'

(Which she did ... in Finchley Road. It is not usual for relatives to accompany persons under arrest in police transport they were obviously doing her a favour).

'THE REFUSAL OF ANY INFORMATION TO
THE PRESS AND OTHER INQUIRERS – EVEN MPS'

Quite normal in such cases.

'A NIGHT AT A POLICE STATION'–

It's the sausage and chips for breakfast that usually breaks them.

'AND THEN QUIET EVICTION
IN THE EARLY MORNING'

(There's that wicked 'early' again).

'ALL ON THE INSTRUCTIONS OF THE HOME OFFICE'

And the news item went on:

> 'Mrs. ———'s only crime, he said, was that she wanted to stay with her children'–

(aged 27, 24, and 15)
> 'in Britain because she had neither country nor home elsewhere.'

According to the *Evening Standard* she had been living in Austria previously and whilst she didn't have a passport she did possess a document issued by the Austrian Government that entitled her to reside in Austria:

> 'Now, in the name of the British people, she had been forcibly separated from her family and sent - with callous indifference – to wander Europe seeking a living and a home. Perhaps had Mrs —— —— been a Spanish stowaway, a Rumanian dancer or a Russian athlete the red carpet might have been laid out in welcome by the Home Office. But there was little propaganda value in a mother's wish to remain with her children. It was not a matter of party politics but Liberals at least would not cease their efforts to reunite the family.'

The quoted statement from the alien herself was somewhat calmer:

> 'Before Leaving London Mrs —— said, "I don't want to go because I like England and do not like Austria much." She hoped to be able to live with her sister in Klagenfurt.'

This *exposé* was topped by a large photograph of the alien boarding the plane escorted by 'OFFICIALS' (those fiends from OGPU again – Frank and I).

The *Daily Express*, incidentally, didn't even think it worth a follow-up the next day. And I didn't see anything further about the Liberals' unceasing efforts.

But no one spotted the real story except my Sarge.

'I see we have our picture in the evening paper,' she said, 'those wouldn't be high heels you are wearing, would they?'

'Where, let me see?' I said playing for time.

When I had ascertained that the photo gave nothing away I said confidently, 'Of course not, Sarge!'

'Where,' she said, pausing dramatically, 'is your hat?'

'Well, that's taken from the front, Sarge – and you know those pill box things stick on the back of your head?' She looked at me slyly.

'Just thought I'd ask you in case someone asked *me*. Of course I knew that you *must* be wearing a hat!'

Fortunately she didn't see the all-revealing picture the following day!

16
Transfer

After three and a half years at West End Central came transfer. I had been expecting it. By now, all the girls who had been at the station when I arrived had either left the job (usually to get married) or transferred (usually because of marriage). I had become the sub-division's old timer – though not the one with the longest service. I knew that one of the girls at Tottenham Court Road had been voluntarily seconded to Cyprus and that I was next in line for a transfer. I could do worse.

I left West End Central with mixed feelings. Whilst I liked working in the area I was becoming a bit bored with frequently taking new girls 'learning beats', a chore naturally reserved for the senior girls. This double responsibility plus the necessity of always being on one's best behaviour (one felt obliged to let them learn their own bad habits) was somewhat wearing. Also I welcomed the idea of being free from the sometimes irksome supervision of the three women Sergeants and an Inspector.

But I had always found Tottenham Court Road nick a depressing place: outside a hideous brick eyesore and inside dark and gloomy. Smaller of course than West End Central with the usual police station eccentricity of layout. They really were the oddest places and no two were alike. Here we had one vast charge room for coping with both male and female prisoners. It swam in a sea of dingy parquet and was surrounded by dirty, cream and brown walls. At the rear of the building was a fairly large, partially covered yard which the 'C' division area cars used as their base. Early morning would see the gum-booted crews sloshing down their chariots.

The women police room on the ground floor was quite large and pleasant enough but the poor lighting made it rather bleak at night.

I was to be on the same relief as Chris (just the two of us) – a big blonde girl with a slightly brusque manner. I was not too pleased about this as we had met at West End Central previously and had disliked each other on sight. But we pretended our antagonism did not exist, grated along on each other's nerves for a while gradually achieving peaceful co-existence and eventually became good friends. I enlisted the aid of her phenomenal memory whilst writing this book.

On the opposite relief were a pleasant girl who soon left to get married – and Heather. Heather was something of a legend throughout the division due to her good looks, sparkle and elegance. Her wardrobe was immense and her taste impeccable. One felt eclipsed when she was around.

Although directly under the supervision of the male station officer we were much freer than at West End Central but had to accept more responsibility being left alone to 'get on with it'. However, the West End Central woman Inspector and women Sergeants paid us frequent 'surprise' visits. If they really *were* a surprise we would complain bitterly to the West End Central reserve girl that she was falling down on her job as early warning system operator! Quite often we would be on duty alone and although the chaps were very nice I did miss the company of our big group of girls (Chris did not share my feelings). On early turn we were often without a matron so if female charges came in we had to cope and stay in.

Like the old, my new ground was sharply divided into two. Tottenham Court Road was the dividing line. On one side, the area bounded by Oxford Street, Upper Regent Street and Euston Road was a jumble of dress factories, wholesale gown showrooms, offices, the vast Middlesex Hospital with its satellite buildings and the BBC. Population-wise, Cypriots (both Greek and Turkish varieties) predominated, then a fair sprinkling of Italians, with a top-up of every nationality under the sun. The restaurants were mainly those of the predominant nationalities with the notable exception of the huge, economical Schmidts. There was a fairly large number of flats ranging from the slum type to a few very elegant ones in the Portland Place area.

The 'other side' was bounded by Euston Road, New Oxford

Street and Russell Square and was devoted to bodily health, mental stimuli and social welfare. The main buildings of London University occupied a central chunk and its numerous colleges, departments and hostels spilled over into much of the rest. Then there was the University College Hospital and its medical school, the British Museum, Congress House (the Trade Union HQ), the Royal Academy of Dramatic Art, the YM and YWCA plus two or three other hostels, the Courtauld Art Gallery and the Percival David Foundation of Chinese Art, numerous society headquarters from the Architectural Association to the Licensed Victuallers Central Protection Society, many publishers, service flats, several hotels, Americans for the use of, and a large block of police flats.

My favourite part was the slice between New Oxford Street and the British Museum with its book and trinket shops – a delightful mixture of erudition and eccentricity. Here one could purchase a genuine Bedouin necklace, volumes on The Nature of Anthroposophy, Nine Lectures on Bees or even The Secrets of Chinese Meditation.

Although my new nick was only across the street (Oxford Street actually) from my previous station, much of our work was very different. Checking up on aliens, interviewing attempted suicides and making many other hospital visits for various reasons now occupied much more of my time.

Even callers at the station differed considerably. Being on a main road close by the big railway termini we received many visits from persons who left home, came to London and then 'found' that they had no money and/or nowhere to go. I thought it incredible that they could just take off like that without any security. It was common to have either an entire family arriving in this way or just the wife and children after a row with the husband. Either he had chucked her out or she had suddenly had enough. One such (whom I could hardly blame) was a woman from the north who arrived at the nick late one evening. Her husband had kept her short of money and generally ill-treated her but the final straw was when he brought his mate home from the club and instructed her to have intercourse with him. Amazingly, she did (obviously terrified of her husband) and the mate paid with 'the change he had on him' nine and eightpence ha'penny. Perhaps it was the eightpence ha'penny that did it.

The main road situation also brought more girls who had 'lost my purse' or had some other excuse for being destitute. Two of these who were not yet seventeen (separate incidents) I had to deal with for Care or Protection because their parents refused to collect them or deposit their fare home.

A grandmother did turn up at the court hearing of one of the girls – a thirteen-year-old. She was fortunate compared with sixteen-year-old Angela from the Midlands. Her mother not only refused to collect her but informed us that she was not prepared to have her home again even if the Court preferred this. No one bothered to turn up for her court appearance. Apparently, Angela had been ousted from her mother's affections by a stepfather who came on the scene when she was ten years old. After leaving school she drifted from job to job, was once arrested for stealing, left home without any objections from her mother and eventually came to London. When she reached me – with a cock and bull story and a year on her age – she was dirty, unkempt and destitute. Trouble was that not only was Angela not very intelligent and a compulsive liar, she also had a rather unpleasant personality which quickly antagonised people.

She wrote to me and asked if I would visit her whilst she was in the remand home. Both Bob and I felt very sympathetic so we spent our only day off (the Met. Police still worked a six day week) driving to the outskirts of London to see her. The woman in charge, though surprised and mystified, greeted us charmingly and gave us tea and cakes. She, too, had found it difficult to like the girl who was behaving in a vindictive and trouble-making fashion. Angela adopted an air of casual arrogance, she lied continuously and paraded us like trophies before the other girls. We decided that our visit had been a mistake; that it was unwise for police officers to get mixed up with so unstable a character and agreed to leave things of this nature to trained social workers in the future. We, too, rejected her.

One unusual 'caller at the station' was a young Jamaican girl with a sorry tale. Her boss had attempted to seduce her and had committed minor sexual assaults against her, pawing her and putting his hands up her clothes, etc. She reported it to the police and preferred a charge thereby losing her job. It was not easy for her to get another. The other employees promised they would back her up but when the case came to Court they all went over to the other side and denied her story. He was found not guilty.

She kept sobbing, 'I thought British Justice was fair.'

She was broken hearted that they had (she alleged) all told lies to save him and thereby made her appear a liar when it was she who was telling the truth. She only wanted justice. But she had come to the obvious conclusion. It had happened like that because he was white and she was black.

And she sat in our bleak waiting-room and cried and cried.

Our general duties among the local residents were also often of a different nature due mainly to the presence of a lower income group and more lonely bed-sits.

Brief examples of incidents that stand out in my memory:

An old woman who kept throwing her belongings out of her upper-storey window to gain attention and so speed up her entry into an old people's home.

A senile, mentally-retarded, but inseparable couple who had not been seen for a couple of days. When we broke into their neglected room we found them in bed. The woman was cuddling and talking to the old man's lifeless body and she refused to be parted from him or to believe that he was dead.

The fourteen-year-old Greek-Cypriot girl who did not fit into any category. She spoke not a word of English, was married, was pregnant and had been abandoned by her husband. Her family was not in this country. The marriage was legal as it had taken place abroad – and this prevented us from dealing with her for Care and Protection. She couldn't go to an adults' hostel, most of the children's places could only accept her if she was being dealt with as a juvenile and the remainder hadn't the facilities to cope with a pregnant, non-English speaker. Eventually, when we were nearly frantic, the dear old Salvation Army came to our aid and welcomed her very kindly to a lovely little hostel near King's Cross station until further arrangements could be made.

A blind old lady whom we found dead when we broke into her room. She lay face-down on the bare floor-boards with a pool of blood by her temple. It looked a bit sinister but we discovered she had collapsed with a heart attack and had struck her head on the fender as she fell. It was an overcast morning so I went to switch on the light but there was no bulb in the socket. Obviously, she didn't need one. But her blindness was to pose a bigger problem when it came to informing next of kin. The neighbours knew little and she had no address book or correspondence. Why should she? In fact the only words to be seen anywhere were her own name and address on a bundle of Braille books. It was Sunday so we had to wait till the following day to enlist the assistance of the organisations for the blind.

A man who for several mornings ran along a turning off Oxford Street. Scarcely breaking step he would smack the bottom of one or other of the girls who was turning into a narrow passageway leading to their place of employment. By the time the shocked female had turned round he had almost disappeared down the street. After several such incidents the girls complained to the nick and special police attention was given. But the slap-happy character returned no more.

A rather unpleasant inter-neighbour incident involving a very well-known member of the cast of the BBC radio serial Mrs Dale's Diary in which she was all sweetness and light. But in real life...

And so on.

17
Hospitals

The young doctor paused on his ward round and nodded in my direction.
'How are we today?'
'Very well, thank you.'
'You're looking much better,' he said reassuringly as he moved on. My charge caught my eye and we collapsed with laughter.

'He thinks you're the dancer from the Pigalle who has the corner bed over there. She's had her appendix out. I must say you do look settled in.'

True. In plain clothes, well ensconced in an armchair and with a magazine on my lap I suppose I didn't give the impression of a Metropolitan Police Officer on hospital observation duty. One can hardly sit to attention for hours and I would have been less alert minus my magazine. But a night club dancer! Flattering anyway.

This particular observation at the Charing Cross Hospital was on a prostitute who had attempted suicide and was one of several such hospital observations I did in Central London. I also graced St George's at Hyde Park Corner, the Middlesex just above Oxford Street and the University College near the British Museum.

Police officers often spend a lot of time in and around hospitals so with two large hospitals on my new sub-division my visits increased. Sometimes we escorted patients there in the ambulance (when there was some difficulty in identification or insufficient time at the scene to take personal details) or attended to take details of accidents reported to the police by the ambulance service or to escort the occasional loss of memory caller at the nick.

We reported accidents of all kinds. One that turned out not to be an accident in our sense of the word concerned a cook in a West End establishment. Quote:

'I was bending down to put a rice pudding in the oven when I felt this agonising pain in my back...' She had a slipped disc.

Full-time hospital observations were kept on certain attempted suicides and any sick or injured prisoner not yet brought before the court. Perhaps because it was lonely bed-sit land that the incidence of attempted suicide on our ground seemed to be particularly high. The accent was on attempted. Success was rare. If any police implementation of a law suffered from great public misunderstanding the 'suicide law' was surely the one. So often I have heard people say, 'Fancy charging a person with attempted suicide. It's their own life' – as if we were out to punish the unfortunates. The point was that in practice they were rarely charged. In the dozens of attempts dealt with by colleagues and myself I can remember only two cases that were taken to Court and one of these was because she kept causing a public nuisance while doing it.

But the threat of being charged did give us power to insist that the attempters agree to us handing them into the care of a relative, friend or social worker, which otherwise they may have been reluctant to do. This course was taken after ensuring that the patients were rational and had at least stated that they would not make a further attempt. We were not naïve enough to believe that they would necessarily keep their word or that their relation or friend would be able to prevent them if they were really determined, but many of these people were lonely and felt unloved. They needed sympathetic human contact but were reluctant (often through pride) to seek it themselves. At least this method was a step in the right direction. Putting them into someone's care also helped to give them a sense of responsibility to others. But if a patient made it clear that they were going to have another try or refused to co-operate they would be charged merely in order to protect them from themselves. This was also the attitude of the Court. Certainly never punitive.

There was a school of thought which insisted that one should have the right to take one's own life. This was all very well if a 'normal' frame of mind existed when the attempt was made. But who's to know? So many attempters seem glad to be alive when they recover.

I once nursed a man who had cut his wrists and throat (but like many people did not know how to do it properly), taken an overdose of drugs and put his head in the gas oven. One might presume he didn't want to live. He was saved, and after a few weeks in hospital, gradually became more cheerful and began to get his problems into perspective. He was most concerned and frightened when one of his wrist wounds began to open up.

Then of course there was the matter of responsibility to the people one involved. Some attempts caused great strain and trouble to others such as relatives, or the unlucky driver of the train in front of which they threw themselves.

If violence was expected or a second suicide attempt seemed likely we kept full-time observation in the hospital. Otherwise the patient usually remained there until sufficiently recovered and rational enough to be interviewed by us. We took a statement and on this, and all other information available, the station officer would decide the best course of action. Loneliness and unhappy love affairs were the chief reasons given for attempts but I think some were just neurotic and inadequate people. The most remarkable reason for an attempt was given me by a patient's fiancée, 'He was very upset yesterday because they (a music school) were trying to make him sing operatic pieces and he would rather sing Neapolitan songs. He is a very nervous type.'

Once, for a couple of weeks, we kept full-time hospital observation on a prisoner not yet brought before the Court. Julie was a twenty-five-year-old prostitute with convictions for larceny, obtaining credit by fraud, possessing dangerous drugs, brothel keeping and false pretences. A nice girl. We gathered that on this occasion, after her arrest for soliciting prostitution, she had reacted violently by attempting to relieve the arresting officer of one of his eyes with her pointed umbrella. In the ensuing melee her jaw which was in the process of mending from a previous fracture was re-fractured. She was additionally charged with assault on the police. Whilst this may sound harsh it's worth remembering that if her umbrella point had found its target the charge could have been a far more serious one.

Now her teeth were wired together to assist the fracture to heal. This didn't stop her from talking. She was interested in clothes and make-up and carefully dissected my appearance (plain clothes) every day. Fortunately she was mainly complimentary.

Julie was one of those cheerfully immoral people. Friendly and easy to get on with when not thwarted but, I suspected, minus any loyalty, scruples or conscience. I didn't trust her an inch.

'Miss B... doesn't follow me to the toilet and everywhere like you do.

She trusts me,' she said, mentioning an over-casual, young WPC.

'She must be mad,' I said feelingly, I wouldn't trust you out of my sight for a second.'

'But I've got no clothes and my teeth are all wired up,' she retorted.

'So?'

She laughed. She agreed with me. It was all part of the game.

With her very black hair and green eyes she was attractive in a slightly coarse way. Her be-muscled 'boy-friend' turned up at visiting time every evening and just about climbed into bed with her while I sat there like a prim peeping torn watching in case he tried to pass her anything. She was a little worried about their prolonged separation.

'He's probably going with somebody else already,' she confided. 'They can't do without it for very long can they?'

I declined to comment.

I collected her on the day she went to Court, teeth still wired but dressed in an expensive, smart suit which showed off her very good figure to perfection. She paraded round very pleased with herself.

'It's my hips that get me most of my customers,' she confided, 'I just swing them like this.' She gave a convincing performance. I trailed after her on her lap of honour like Little Orphan Annie behind the 'It' girl. She gravitated instinctively to the adjoining men's ward. I stood in the ward doorway and watched her performance.

'What's she doing in there?' asked a passing nurse.

'Just acquiring a few new customers,' I answered casually.

'Good heavens, she's not, is she?' she exclaimed, taking me quite literally. She was really shocked.

I made a mental note to curb my warped police humour in the presence of young innocents.

In court, Julie was sentenced to four months and departed to Holloway Prison. They returned her to the outside hospital for further treatment but did not put a prison guard on her. Two days later she walked out, teeth still wired (and supposed to remain so for a further four weeks) and wearing her dressing gown. She was last seen hailing a taxi. I don't know if she was ever apprehended – certainly not during the ensuing three months, after which I left.

18
A Lovely Pair of Fur Boots

'A baby has been abandoned in my church!'

The voice on the telephone sounded disconcerted.

When Chris and I arrived shortly afterwards the baby was still sleeping peacefully in the pew where she had been found. A large, heavy chair had been placed in front to prevent her rolling off.

'The chair wasn't in its usual place and when I went to move it I saw the baby,' said the rather boyish vicar who was obviously stunned by this sudden crisis.

She was a pretty infant, healthy looking and well wrapped in woollies, a baby's plastic mac and a short, white nylon fur coat. Beside her was an almost empty feeding bottle.

'I've asked around to see if anyone saw a mother and baby, and looked outside for a pram but no luck,' said the vicar. 'It couldn't have been here long without being noticed. The church is well frequented and the verger or myself are nearly always here.'

We took the baby to the Middlesex Hospital where she was examined, changed and fed. Then back to the station while we arranged nursery accommodation. Her clothing revealed nothing except the name 'Harris' written in Indian ink on one of her three vests. We estimated she was about six months old.

Word of 'our baby' soon got around and the whole station staff managed to find an excuse to visit the women police office. They cooed and baby-talked, gave us poor, childless women authoritative advice on baby care and generally approved our age estimate of six months. Baby loved all the attention. She gurgled at the silver whistles and keys proffered by the PCs and dribbled happily down immaculate Inspectors' serge.

We placed her in a cheerful LCC nursery in North London and set the identification ball rolling. A circular giving a very detailed description of babe and clothing was sent to all divisions requesting that enquiries be made at all clinics and hospitals with special emphasis on the name 'Harris'. Photographs were issued to the Press.

The circular unearthed a surprising number of women named 'Harris' who had had recent confinements. All were seen and asked to produce their babies. One mother had loaned baby clothes to a girl named Franks whilst in a home for unmarried mothers. When we found Miss Franks her baby had been 'taken into care' and was being adopted.

Police in the East End remembered a prostitute named 'Harris' who had been pregnant twelve months before, but were unable to trace her.

The press photo brought forth a few people who thought they recognised the baby (they were all mistaken) and one pathetic letter from a woman asking that she be given the child and pointing out that she was also in the market for a baby boy should we happen to find one.

About a week later Chris took the baby to the Juvenile Court as being in need of Care or Protection. A four-week interim order was made so that enquiries could continue. More mums eliminated themselves from investigations by showing their babies to police. A further four-week order was made at the next appearance but all our enquiries produced negative results.

At the termination of the second order the case was found proved and a lighter note was introduced into the court proceedings when the baby was given a name and date of birth (making her now exactly eight months) by the magistrates.

Enquiries petered out. We had exhausted all avenues. It seemed that the rest of the story, as so often in that job, would remain a mystery. Involved as we were with alien enquiries, attempted suicides, etc., our baby faded into the background and was eventually forgotten.

Three and a half months later we had a phone call from Hyde Park nick.

'We've got a woman here who says she left a baby in a church on your ground. I haven't checked the records yet. Know anything about it?'

As I walked into Hyde Park police station my curiosity was rekindled, wondering what to expect. I certainly didn't expect Jeannie Black. She was twenty, Irish and straight from the bogs. Her straight, black, pudding-basin-cut hair framed a scrubbed, waif-like face with large dark eyes. A child-woman. My animosity faded in the face of her incredible naivety coupled with that odd, not-quite-of-this-world Irish charm. She seemed to be more sinned against than sinning.

'Why,' I said severely when I first saw her, 'did you decide to come forward after all this time?'

'Well,' she said patiently, 'I was sitting on this bench in the park thinking about my baby, like I often do, when along comes this policeman and suddenly the Good Lord says to me, "Go and tell him all about it" – so I did.'

'All about it' was as follows:

Both she and her husband had been ejected from their rented rooms after other tenants had complained about the baby crying. They were unable to find accommodation where the baby would be accepted and the husband had lost his job as a coffee stall attendant when he took time off to help Jeannie search. Whilst wandering around destitute they saw the church and her husband decided to leave the baby there – otherwise they would never find rooms. Jeannie protested and she cried but he was insistent so she wrapped the baby in her coat and left it in the pew.

'Freddie chose a Protestant church so they wouldn't suspect us,' she confided, obviously impressed by this reasoning.

Getting a room was now easy. Next day, Jeannie saw the baby's photograph in the paper and wanted to claim her but Freddie said they would get into trouble. He didn't find another job but told her she must earn some money by going 'on the game' in Hyde Park.

'I told him *he* ought to get a job and keep us but he gave me a hiding for saying that,' she said without rancour.

She started soliciting but would only stay out for short periods and earned a pound or thirty shillings in an evening. She told Freddie that the police kept moving her on but he suspected she was exaggerating. He took to watching from outside the park and sent her back if she came out too soon.

'It's horrible, some of the men want to kiss you as well but I don't let them do that,' she said with a note of pride, 'it makes me feel sick. Trouble is it sometimes puts me off going with poor Freddie. He gets furious and says I don't love him, but I do.'

She admitted that she sometimes doubted his affection when he kept sending her back to solicit in the cold weather.

But he loves me really,' she hastened to reassure me. 'He bought me a lovely pair of fur boots to keep my feet warm in the park. He's very good to me.'

I looked incredulously at her simple, open face. She really meant it!

'I often grumbled at Freddie and told him that I missed our baby but he just said he missed her too and wouldn't let me go and get her back.'

It was decided that a charge of abandonment could not be substantiated as there had to be proof that the baby was not likely to be found and could have come to some harm. Chris took a statement, then referred Jeannie to the Children's Officer in charge of the baby's case.

'All I want now is for both of us to get a job so we can have the baby back,' she said.

I would like to have seen the husband charged with 'Living on immoral earnings' but our only evidence was Jeannie's and she would have retracted immediately to save her beloved Freddie.

Next day, the National Assistance Board telephoned to inform us that the Blacks had been interviewed and had been sent to separate hostels where the Superintendents had undertaken to find them work.

After a lull of several months the Children's Officer telephoned to enquire if we knew the whereabouts of Jeannie and Freddie.

'The baby had to be taken away from very good foster parents who wanted to adopt her but the Blacks turned up saying they wanted to reclaim her. Now they've disappeared again but I can't return the baby while things are so uncertain. It's a rotten shame. The foster parents are very upset. It's the second time they've had a baby taken away.'

We were unable to assist not having heard of the Blacks since the message from the National Assistance Board.

About a year later I was at Chelsea Juvenile Court when I saw Jeannie sitting among the parents and children awaiting court appearance. She was holding a tiny baby in her arms. It was not *the* baby. She recognised me immediately.

'Did you get your other baby back?' I asked.

'Well, no,' she blushed. 'We were going to but my husband lost his job and he's in prison now. I would like her back one day,' she added wistfully.

I read the riot act to her about her selfishness and irresponsibility whilst she looked suitably chastened and promised to get in touch with the Children's Officer. But I scarcely scraped her wall of incomprehension.

'You've had another baby? What are you doing here with it?' I asked.

'Oh no, it's not mine!' she laughed. 'His mother asked me to look after him one day and then she didn't come back! I just came along to sit with him because I didn't like to think of him here all on his own. Poor little thing – being left like that.'

My God, would you credit it?

19
'I Do Not Understand'

Aliens came into my life in a big way at Tottenham Court Road. They lived and worked in the area in large numbers. The hospitals employed them as domestic labour, the restaurants as cooks and waiters and in the posher parts they were taken on as au pairs. Also, quite a number lived in bed-sits locally.

Any change of address, employment or marital status was supposed to be notified to police but of course many aliens neglected to do this or 'did not understand'.

We had a regular flow of alien enquiries allotted to each of us which mainly amounted to chasing up these omissions. After groping around in the dark for a while I eventually acquired a new skill – 'reading' the stamps and endorsements on aliens' registration cards and passports and understanding the terms and regulations pertaining to aliens.

We also interviewed those who had requested cancellation or variations of landing conditions such as extensions of stay or permission to obtain other work.

I rather enjoyed preparing these reports for the Home Office. They were of a more personal nature, were necessarily in narrative form rather than officialese and – luxury of luxuries – we were even asked in some cases to express an opinion or at least were expected to intimate by the manner of our reports the validity of the aliens' requests or excuses.

The Home Office enquiries covered a wide field. On one occasion I had to investigate a report that an Italian was suspected of having procured a criminal abortion (found to be false). On another I was obliged to look thoroughly into the financial affairs of a young woman who wished to support an Austrian girl through Art School – the alien had been very kind to her mother when an au pair.

It was good to meet an au pair and a family who were happy with each other. Too often an alien would complain that she was given too much work and many employers thought their au pair lazy. There were certainly faults on both sides. Many of the aliens came from 'good families' and resented or were not used to any sort of work especially menial, whilst some English women regarded an au pair as a very economical drudge.

I found one particular inquiry most amusing. It requested that I enquire of a German girl whether she had obtained Ministry of Labour permission for her apparent change of employment and what in fact that employment was. She had registered a change of address at our station and her employment had been noted as 'gymnastic help'. Was this perhaps something to do with physiotherapy? Well, the term was new to me. I'd never come across it in hospital.

The Sergeant who had registered the change was no wiser so I visited the alien at a luxurious flat in Portland Place. The owners assured me that the girl was merely a resident domestic. I interviewed her alone to see what sort of hanky-panky was going on. She was puzzled, insisting she had done nothing wrong and had permission for her job. Her English was poor and her accent thick.

But you've changed your employment,' I insisted.

'No, no.'

'What work are you doing then?'

I had to ask her to repeat the answer twice. Then I got it: 'Domestic help.'

'What else?'

'Nothing else, just domestic help.'

Slowly the light began to dawn.

'Say it again,' I asked.

Thickly, gutturally, for the mad English she said, 'Domestic help.'

Of course! Phonetically it sounded like 'gymnastic help' and might well be taken as that by anyone not good at understanding heavily accented English (I became very adept though I have no flair for languages).

What really amused me was the way the report had gone through the usual channels without query until it was found that the employment did not match up with the permission given. No one had had the nerve to say, 'The King has got no clothes'.

Sometimes, aliens came to our notice in other ways. In answer to a telephone call one spring morning I went to a small hotel near the BBC. The proprietor told me that one of the two young German girls he employed as domestics had become mentally unbalanced and the other had gone missing. Their work had been unsatisfactory from the beginning and they were both very lazy. They also appeared to be carrying on a lesbian relationship and were frequently involved in emotional scenes and rows. These terminated in an exceptionally violent row two nights before during which one of them (Schmidt) had become hysterical. The following morning the other girl (Hauptmann) – from her photo, pretty but hard-faced – had left, refusing to say where she was going and leaving all her luggage behind. She had not returned. Schmidt had now become seriously mentally disturbed, wandering around naked and quite uncontrollable.

The hotelier tried frantically to keep her away from his guests and called in the German Welfare Officer who eventually acquired the services of the DAO. He promptly 'deemed her to be of unsound mind' and placed her in a mental hospital.

The room the girls had occupied was in a dreadful state. Furniture awry, clothing flung around, German words written on the wall in lipstick, and urine stains on the bed and the adjoining wall.

I contacted the Alien Traffic Index and was informed that Hauptmann had left the UK via Dover the previous day – obviously she had gone straight there from the hotel. I passed this information on to the Aliens Registration Office.

Six weeks later the Home Office asked us for a report about the girls. I visited the hotel again to bring myself up to date. Ten days after her dramatic walk-out Hauptmann had returned to collect some of her luggage. Schmidt, much improved, had been released about a fortnight after her breakdown. She had requested her old job back but, rather understandably, the hotel 'did not feel inclined to re-employ her'. She returned to Germany in the care of the Welfare Officer and took the remainder of Hauptmann's luggage with her. Apparently the cause of her breakdown was that Hauptmann had become attracted to a boy she had met in Paris. This had caused a lot of trouble between them and when she left to go to the boy, the shock had proved too much for Schmidt, it being 'the first big shock of her adult life'.

So, although I did many enquiries and reports about these girls, I never saw either of them.

A considerable number of aliens ended up in our cells charged with shoplifting. We often escorted them from the store after they had been detained by the store detective and at the station we assisted generally in the charging procedure and enquiries. The popular picture of a shoplifter seemed to be that of a lonely, middle-aged woman seeking affection. Our average shoplifter was an intrepid young female alien looking for something for nothing.

It was of course *the* female crime. The only one in which we indulged heavily and we tried hard to make up for our tardiness in other fields.

Well over half of our shoplifters were aliens. Almost all nationalities were represented with the French leading the field whilst the Italians and Spanish came close seconds (of course this was partly due to there being more of those nationalities in the UK). Among foreign visitors who came here in any great numbers the North American seemed to be the least likely to commit this offence (I can remember only one) but to get the true picture one would have to get a complete breakdown of the numbers of each nationality present at any one time and their length of stay. One thing *was* clear the offence is neither confined to natives of poorer countries nor to those with no money in their pockets.

The familiar pattern with the shoplifter was as follows. The store detective would spot them 'at it' and follow them around but never approach them until they had left the store. This was to prove that they had no intention of paying before they left – a familiar defence. Once in the street they would be stopped and asked to come to the manager's office. We would then be informed by telephone. On our arrival we would listen to the evidence of the store detective and if sufficient to sustain a charge the alleged offender would be formally arrested and taken to the nick.

The reaction of shoplifters on our arrival at the store and later at the station seems to set the Briton apart from most aliens. With the latter an emotional scene was almost inevitable. Weeping, wailing, beating of breasts, being sorry (that they were caught), offers to pay, pleading whilst grabbing at our sleeves and even getting down on their knees to beseech and tug at our skirts.

Their attitude that *we* were bringing all this trouble on *them* did not make them any more endearing.

One day a young Persian woman and her mother were brought in together with their very young baby in a pram. They had been 'well at it' and had piles of stolen items in shopping bags. We took the baby into the women police office whilst the charge was being preferred. Busily attending to the baby we almost forgot to look in the pram. This would have been a grave error for well concealed between two mattresses were three pairs of briefs, two petticoats, one brooch, and two pairs of leather gloves all complete with price tags!

The women were from a wealthy family and had come over here for the younger one to have her baby. Persian female shoplifters varied from the others in one respect – they nearly always plead not guilty. (It was reputed that they could be automatically divorced in disgrace by their husbands if convicted of stealing.)

I never ceased to be amazed at the nerve of some shoplifters. Not content with getting away with it once they would continue from store to store. When caught, goods from three or four stores would be found on them. Others would 'lift' a shopping bag first in which to put all the other 'lifted' goods. Recently, a woman found that an expensive beauty-case had been attached to the counter with nylon cords – to thwart the likes of her. Not to be outdone she went to another department, stole a pair of scissors, returned, cut the cords and made off with her prize! She was arrested. Some thieves even have the nerve to take stolen goods to the refund desk to obtain a cash 'return'.

Of course we did get the odd, genuinely pathetic case like the little old lady who lifted a hat, promptly wore it in place of her own but omitted to remove the price tag and wandered round the store with it dangling obviously down her back.

20
Not Been Seen Since

Another person reported missing – a regular occurrence. An adult too. We *did* make an effort to trace missing adults but they very often left their residence quite intentionally and didn't want to be traced.

This one, however, had apparently left all her clothes and personal belongings behind. Also, she was thought to have left the hostel where she resided at some time between nine-thirty in the evening and midnight. Not a very good time to start a new life minus personal belongings. She *could* have gone to see friends on the spur of the moment. But then again it was five nights since she had left – long enough to ratify an impulsive departure. A bit dodgy.

Frances was a twenty-three-year-old school teacher from Scotland. She taught in a secondary school in London's East End and lived in a permanent hostel. The warden reported her missing, fairly forgivably, five days after she was thought to have departed. Girls who live in Central London hostels are a bit apt to come and go, visit relatives, etc., without prior warning.

'It's not like her to do this she's a nice, quiet, sensible girl,' said the warden.

'Any friends I could talk to?'

'Well no, she isn't very close to anyone here. But there are the two girls who pointed out that she was missing. They saw her last.'

I found the two girls pleasant but a little prim. They had seen Frances at supper about nine o'clock on the evening of her presumed departure. The hostel closed at midnight and she had not been seen the following day. She had appeared perfectly normal that evening and didn't seem worried about anything. Somehow I had the feeling they were a bit uneasy and that they rather disapproved of Frances.

I searched her room which certainly seemed to contain all her belongings including oceans of correspondence and notebooks containing some rather introspective scribbling. It was difficult to ascertain what she was wearing when she left. She had lots of clothes, was a hoarder in fact, and no one knew her well enough to say what was missing. The two girls gave me a description of what she had been wearing when they had talked to her at supper but these clothes were still in her room.

But most important – I found an address book and a recent photograph. She looked a typical Scot. Dark, curly hair framed a strong-featured, intelligent face. I was told she had a strong Scottish accent. There was, I was informed, a close friend who lived in Kensington who might be able to help me more.

An odd one this, an air of foreboding about it. Probably my imagination. She'd turn up in a couple of days with a perfectly rational explanation like so many did. After all she had been quite normal that evening, not worried about anything.

I circulated her as a missing person and checked whether there were any unidentified persons found who might match up.

Enquiries at her school produced nothing. They had no idea where she might have gone and had heard nothing from her. She was not in any trouble there, her work was quite satisfactory. She was not at her parents' home in Aberdeen. She was not with her friend Jean in Kensington. Jean, a pleasant, kindly woman of over thirty was most distressed to hear of her disappearance.

I began to plough my way through her address book trying to pick out the important ones first. But of course the ones that look important so often aren't.

A couple of nights later the two hostel girls appeared at the nick and asked to see me. They had something to tell me, they explained, looking rather abashed. Frances *had* been very upset the night she disappeared – distraught in fact. She had opened her heart to them as follows:

At a party she had recently attended she had had rather too much to drink. She remembered nothing about the latter part of the evening but had woken up next morning to find herself in bed with an Irishman whom she had never seen before. She was worried to death that she might be pregnant and was talking of leaving that evening and going home to Aberdeen. They had dissuaded her from this course. They didn't know why she had chosen to reveal this to them as they weren't close friends but they felt they ought not to 'tell on her' unless it was absolutely necessary. She had clearly shocked them. Inwardly, I cursed their prissiness.

'Of course this puts a very different complexion on things. I think it's quite likely she's lost her memory or more probably committed suicide,' I said brutally, trying to shock them out of their smug complacency. But I was wasting my time.

Her good friend Jean admitted that Frances had spoken to her about the party incident but received the impression that she was more worried about the possibility of VD than pregnancy. Jean was heartbroken that she had not paid more attention at the time – 'I was so busy and just didn't realise she was taking it so seriously.'

Back to the address book with a vengeance. I seemed to be in touch with every police force in the country. A wider picture of Frances was being built up.

'She is restless and ambitious, not really satisfied with the everyday job of a school teacher.'

'A pleasant, easy-going girl.'

'Very self-confident.'

'She's unsure of herself -- a bit mixed up.'

It was like one of those stories where everyone sees the person in a different light and all of them are probably right. I was slowly getting to know Frances and becoming quite fond of her, frailties and all. If she had lost her memory or had had an accident she would have turned up as a person found by now. On the other hand, if she had committed suicide where was the body? Even if she had thrown herself in the river surely she would have floated to the top by now?

'Not necessarily,' said a CID officer whom I'd kept informed in case of the possibility of foul play, 'sometimes they get stuck behind a moored barge or something and don't come to light for weeks. They're a bit on the high side by then too.'

Sixteen days after she had gone missing her photograph and a short informative column appeared in a leading national daily.

'Scotland Yard detectives are searching for...'

Oh well, it was a new title for me.

I had exhausted all avenues of inquiry with no result. No one had seen her since the fateful evening. I hoped she hadn't done anything silly for such slender reasons. I wished I could talk to her and tell her it didn't matter – nothing mattered *that* much.

Frances had been gone for four weeks when I received a phone call from a Thames Division officer.

'We've got a body out of the water that *might* be your Frances – though I don't think this body's been in the water for four weeks. Can't tell anything from the description at the moment. Do you know what she was wearing? Or can you check with someone if she had these clothes?'

He gave the details. No one had mentioned them but Jean would know best I supposed. Making this sort of inquiry on the telephone wasn't really done but I thought it unlikely that it was Frances and was doubtful whether Jean could place the clothes for certain.

I got Jean straight away.

'Just a routine inquiry,' I said, 'could you tell me if Frances possessed any of the following?'

Jean was eager as ever to assist.

'A black and blue mixture coat?'

'Yes,' she said without hesitation.

'A blue nightdress?'

'Yes.'

My heart was beginning to sink.

Wine-coloured boots?'

'Yes' – just as promptly but in a small flat voice. She was no fool.

Oh my God, it *was* her. How was I going to tell the poor woman? I couldn't leave her in suspense now.

'Can you tell me why you want to know this?' she said with controlled calm.

I had to have a breathing space.

'Can you hold on a minute, please, I've got someone on the other line.'

I returned to the other phone and told the Thames officer. He asked me to arrange for someone to come and identify the body the following morning. I decided not to ask Jean, she cared too much.

I took a deep breath, arranged my thoughts, picked up the phone and plunged.

'I'm very sorry, my dear, but it's bad news.'

'Go ahead,' she said levelly, 'it's all right.'

'I'm afraid a body wearing those clothes has been found in the Thames.'

There was a short silence.

'I see,' she said finally but without any trace of surprise. She had been expecting this all along but was nursing a hope which I had now taken away from her.

'Of course we don't know for certain,' I said gently, 'she is to be identified in the morning and I'll let you know straight away. But I really don't think there's much doubt.'

'No, I understand, thank you for telling me,' she murmured. She rang off. A short while later she rang back.

'I was wondering if you'd like me to come and identify her. I'll be all right.' She was rallying fast and I had to admire her.

'No, that won't be necessary, we'll get someone from the hostel.'

The hostel warden herself offered to go and as it was my day off Chris accompanied her. But conclusive identification of the body was not possible in this manner and it was eventually done by examining the teeth.

What I wondered about and will never know was how she got down to the river – the nearest spot was about a mile away.

Did an unsuspecting taxi-driver take her? But surely he wouldn't drop an obviously distraught girl by the river without a backward glance? But maybe she didn't look distressed and she could have got out of the cab anywhere. Or maybe she walked through the streets in her nightie, coat and boots. If so, how distressed she must have been not to have changed her mind during that time. Did she really do it for such minor reasons? We shall never know and it makes me very sad to think of it again.

At the inquest, it was disclosed that she was virgo intacta.

21
Goodbye to the Job

So this is the lady policeman's story? Not quite. Only a small part really. There are dozens of other memories...

Making hundreds of beds in the basement gym of Trenchard Section House for police drafted in from the Home Counties during the rail strike of 1955. What with the extra men and a twelve hour day for all of us, Central London was covered in a layer of navy blue.

A policeman asking me the way to the station! Also during the rail strike. His normal venue was the Isle of Wight.

Getting lost at three in the morning in that maze of the old New Scotland Yard (not the new New Scotland Yard) and eventually finding myself in the Press Room where the amused occupants were delighted to show me the way out! I had gone there to collect a photograph of a Borstal escapee who still denied that the perfect likeness was her.

Attending the revival of Mayfair's May Fair when a rich, elderly American gentleman decided that I was just the typically British souvenir he'd been looking for and promptly asked me to go back to the States with him.

The PC on night duty who frequently knocked on a butcher's shop window when a large black cat would appear in the space behind the glass and in front of the internal blind. As pussy made her yawning stretching entrance he would yell, 'Give that cat a spotlight!' beam his torch on her and cheer wildly!

The American serviceman who, to amuse his friends, flung himself on his knees in front of my colleague and me, clasped his hands beseechingly and begged, 'Arrest me, please arrest me!'

We dealt with him in best British fashion by faintly raising our eyebrows, walking round him whilst continuing our conversation and paying him no further attention. Naturally we didn't look back but I bet he felt foolish kneeling in the middle of a crowded pavement in Leicester Square.

Ducks in Hyde Park at dawn rushing from their island nesting place when the crew alighted from an area car to give them their morning feed!

The expression of horror on the face of a travel agency counter clerk in Venice when he saw the occupation of myself and colleague on our passports. He called all his mates over and we had to endure their stares, expressions of disgust and disbelief and mercifully unintelligible comments before we could get our travellers' cheques changed. This was typical of the reaction of most Mediterranean males. The thought that a mere woman should have any sort of authority sent them into paroxysms of rage.

On the same holiday being escorted to the train at Milan station, our baggage carried and the best seats found by three Italian policemen. One of them had been pursuing me around the buffet trailer – in true Italian fashion – and we thought to frighten him off or at least surprise him by announcing we were polizia in Londra. But we reckoned without the international police *esprit de corps*. There was an amazing reversal of the usual attitude. He was absolutely delighted and summoned all *his* mates not to jeer but to greet us warmly and be equally delighted at this amazing phenomenon. They gave us the Royal treatment and waved our train away (much impressing the other occupants) with pleas that we write to them.

Being surrounded by a group of Geordies in Piccadilly Circus when they discovered that I hailed from the same hideous pit village.

'Whey y'bugger, whey y'bugger!' one of them repeated loudly whilst the rest slapped me on the back.

'Come and have a drink then, hen,' one invited.

'No man, she canna,' said another, 'she's wearin' her armband – that means she's on duty.'

Fighting for my 'honour' when cloistered for several hours with a middle-aged woman 'of unsound mind'. She would keep trying to lift my skirt 'to see what you've got on underneath'.

Shepherding potential women recruits through their tests, medical examinations and selection boards and comforting the many who did not get through. The gradual weeding-out created a mounting tension so that final rejection often produced floods of tears. It was something of an honour to be chosen for this task as the hierarchy knew just how thoroughly we were inspected and dissected by the applicants and we had to be duly scrubbed and polished for the occasion.

Being catapulted into the path of Robert Mitchum's car when women behind me were suddenly overcome at the proximity of that sexy hunk and tried to get at him. The PC who dragged me to safety and I was perilously close – had performed a similar service when the crowd gained temporary control at a pop idol's jamboree.

'I won't always be there, you know,' he warned, shaking his finger at me with mock sternness.

A drunk lying full length on the floor of a cafe at nine one morning. He amiably attained the perpendicular at our request and stared down at us from his immense height. He was baby-faced, wore a dinner suit and was obviously left over from last night's party. He quickly regained a fair degree of composure and was such a lovable, trusting drunk that we hadn't the heart to arrest him! We propped him against a wall, threatened dire consequences if he moved a muscle, then hailed a willing cabbie. Once inside he pulled down the window, grabbed my hand and kissed it.

'I must see you again, what's your phone number?' he burbled urgently as the cab pulled away.

We felt very naughty but rather pleased with ourselves. Of course I *did* arrest several people for being drunk and incapable – one of whom was ungrateful enough to knock my hat into the gutter after deciding to 'see if I can escape'. He nearly did.

Pounding the beat with two large, middle-aged, German women police officers in tow. Being the West End (and therefore the showpiece station) we were often visited by women police and social workers from other countries and sometimes took them on patrol with us (walking discreetly a few paces behind). I had this task several times and like the other girls – did not enjoy it much. We felt obliged to 'make something happen' but if we did 'a stop' it was irritating both to us and the stopped girl to have two apparent civilians standing close by and listening in. This would also encourage others to try it and soon we would have what we always tried to avoid an attentive, inquisitive crowd.

A few comments from my public:

'If the officer does not come in out of the rain the officer's hair will come out of curl!' (A Mayfair type being friendly).

A French connoisseur:
'I do not think much of your prostitutes.' *(My* prostitutes!)

'What are you, ma'am?' (American sailors hitting London for the first time).

'Are you in the Salvation Army, then?' (American sailors hitting London for the first time).
'What time do you finish work?' (American sailors...).

Startled Italian to my male colleague:
'I have just seen a woman dressed up as a policeman!' (Me).

And so on.

But of course there is a limit to the number of anecdotes one can cram into a book (I must be joking) and recall is not total, especially in an incident-packed career. For example, although my quoted 'baby found' case is etched on my memory as on crystal I can remember nothing at all about another such case which is mentioned in some old papers of mine.

Letters kept by my mother because 'I knew that one day you would write a book' have served to jog my memory but they also contain mention of incidents that are lost in the haze of time.

Similarly stories recounted at the time to Mother.

'You must put in about the time a man threw his wife and five children out and you couldn't get them in anywhere as it was very late. You were frantic and then had the brain-wave to go and ask the husband to take them back for the night and then chuck them out again in the morning if he must.'

—But I can't, Mum, I don't remember a thing about it. Besides on reflection it seems the obvious thing to do!

I left the Metropolitan Police after nearly six years, partly due to the incompatibility of shifts after marriage and partly because I'm a restless soul.

There have been many changes since I left. Within the last few years the Metropolitan Police have woken up to the twentieth century and have commenced much experimentation and reform.

Panda cars, walkie-talkie radios for beat PCs, the appointment of a PRO, a new 'Yard', and more young blood being promoted are just some of the changes. Divisional boundaries have been altered – my old Tottenham Court Road nick is no longer on 'C'. Better training methods (more practical and less parrot-like learning), and the issue of handy pocket memory aids lessen the confusion in the new police officer's mind.

Care or Protection proceedings are now effected in consultation with the Children's Officer. Police no longer have to attend Court to give evidence in trivial cases – unless the defendant pleads not guilty.

The Street Offences Act has done a good job clearing vice from the streets even though the 'do-gooders' next bind was 'Is it good to drive them underground?' and 'What will they do now?'

Traffic Wardens, parking meters and much towing away have almost eliminated my Soho nightmare of jammed side-streets.

But some new problem always replaces the old. Drugs – not at all serious in my time – are now 'big' in the West End and indeed a matter for concern throughout the country.

But I mustn't forget to mention that most enlightened reform women police may now go bare-headed when in plain clothes!

Did I enjoy it? Well, half of the time I was right in my element and the other half way out of my depth. One of the predominant emotions I remember was fear. Not of being injured but of failing. Being made to look foolish and letting the side down by not being able to control a situation or dig the required plan of action out of the morass of information implanted in my (not very receptive) mind by the training school.

Another, the feeling of being trapped inside the identity of 'a police officer' so that anything I did reflected not on me but on 'the job'. Thus on leaving I felt a great sense of release and freedom – and also regret at not belonging any more.

To sum up I found it boring, interesting, frightening, amusing, infuriating, demanding, easy, thankless and rewarding.

An experience!

Author's Note

Lady Policeman, originally published in 1968, was my first book and attracted quite a lot of media attention (two television interviews and magazine serialisation) chiefly due to the public's curiosity about women police.

Naturally the language used and incidents described in the book were of their time. Black people were called 'coloured' then and when I described Soho as being gay it was in the old-fashioned sense of the word i.e. 'lively, bright, colourful'. At the time policewomen were far from equal but, as they posed little threat, there was little antagonism particularly in the West End which was mostly policed by single young men. (Women police could not enter the specialist branches, few could join the CID and they could certainly not compete with men for promotion.).

My second book was about my earlier training as a nurse. Then, in a moment of madness, I decided to write a book on the history of the British women police. I did not realise how difficult this would be as first in the field particularly given such a fragmented and complex subject and my total lack of research experience. It took me three solid years of hard work to produce *The British Policewoman*: *Her Story* and a BBC Radio 4 Saturday Night Theatre play, *Against All Natural Instincts,* which depicted an early incident in their history.

Once done, I became 'the authority' and for the next twenty years writers, academics, journalists, students, television researchers and schoolgirls beat a path to my door. By the time of women police integration in the mid-1970s I was already writing features on them for the leading police journal (*Police Review*) who then asked me to contribute a regular page to support the women, some of whom were having a very bad time due to male antagonism. I continued writing features asking questions such as why there were not more women detectives/dog handlers and chief constables, and compiled a BBC Radio 4 documentary in which current women police described their integration experiences.

Other writers, mostly academics, began to tackle women police history, some very well. More women police wrote interesting books on their experiences and the television drama *Prime Suspect* brought much attention to the plight of women officers who had been fighting for equality.

For the 100th anniversary of women police in 2015 Hale updated my history in paperback and ebook and I advised on and appeared in a well-received BBC4 TV documentary: *A FAIR COP: A Hundred Years of Women Police*.

It is a very long time since this Lady Policeman patrolled London's West End. Recently, when pointing out to a friend the church in which the abandoned baby girl had been found, she said, 'Your baby would be about sixty years old now.' A sobering thought. I hope she did well. And when I was filmed retracing my steps around Soho for A FAIR COP I was surprised to see how gay, in the newer sense of the word, parts of Soho had become largely due, I was told, to the power of the pink pound.